CU00542470

SECRET
STRATFORD-UPON-AVON

Nicholas Fogg
with photographs from Richard Morris

AMBERLEY

First published 2017

Amberley Publishing
The Hill, Stroud, Gloucestershire, GL5 4EP
www.amberley-books.com

Copyright © Nicholas Fogg, 2017

The right of Nicholas Fogg to be identified as the
Author of this work has been asserted in accordance
with the Copyrights, Designs and Patents Act 1988.

ISBN 978 1 4456 5662 5 (print)
ISBN 978 1 4456 5663 2 (ebook)

British Library Cataloguing in Publication Data.
A catalogue record for this book is available from the
British Library.

Origination by Amberley Publishing.
Printed in Great Britain.

Contents

4

1. The Toll House on the Bridge

In the late fifteenth century Stratford-upon-Avon was fortunate to possess a great benefactor in Sir Hugh Clopton. His greatest gift to the town was the 'great and sumptuous bridge upon the Avon' – a wonder of fourteen arches, and over 400 yards long with its causeway. John Leland, the sixteenth-century antiquary, noted its benefits: 'Before the time of Sir Hugh Clopton there was but a poor bridge of timber and no causeway to come up to it, whereby many poor folks either refused to come to Stratford when the river was up, or coming thither stood in jeopardy of life.'

Clopton Bridge faced its hazards. In 1588 the storms that swept away the Spanish Armada had their effect on the Avon. The floods were so high that when three men crossing the bridge reached the middle, they could not go no further. 'Then, returning presently, could not get back, for the water was so risen. It rose a yard every hour from eight to four.'

During the Civil War Stratford's position as an undefended crossing point of the Avon ensured involvement on the fringes of the conflict. Early in 1645 a brigade of 560 Royalists rode into the town alleging that the townsfolk supported Parliament and demanded £560 to refrain from plunder. There were shrewd bargainers around, for the Cavaliers took off after settling for £10. After this, Parliament ordered that an arch of the bridge be broken down for 'securinge the county and preventinge the incursions of our enemies'.

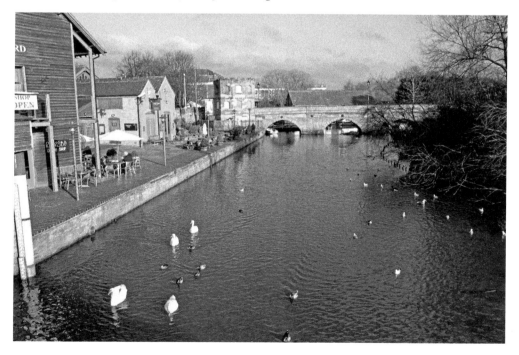

The toll house.

In the early years of the nineteenth century the coaching trade through Stratford reached its zenith, carrying the *Irish Mail* between London and Holyhead. A great deal of the limited prosperity of this impoverished town depended upon it. Yet the continuity of this vital lifeline was inhibited by the condition of the ancient bridge, which was 'narrow, dilapidated and very incommodious for the Travelling and Posing Business'. Richard Wyatt, a 'skilful architect', reported that the old bridge could be widened, but financial considerations prompted a caution increased by the reluctance of any authority to accept responsibility for it. To cover the costs, in 1813, the right to collect tolls on the bridge was auctioned to Thomas Keen for the huge sum of £535. The bridge was widened on the upstream side in 1814, a toll gate was installed and a ten-sided castelled toll house built. Its style reflected the neo-Gothic taste of the age. Despite the improvement, Stratford's Corporation petitioned Parliament for permission to demolish the bridge and erect a new one in the following year. In 1815 the Crown won an action at Leicester Assizes, charging the Corporation with 'the non-repair of a bridge'. A further petition for demolition was prepared, but the old edifice passed precariously to posterity.

The sound of the coach horn and the clatter of horses' hooves on the pebble road drew the Stratfordians to their doors to view the progress of the various stagecoaches, but such events were too frequent to arouse more than brief interest. First in view at 6 a.m. was the *Regent* coach from London en route for Birmingham, Wolverhampton, Shrewsbury and Holyhead. In the next three hours, there followed the *Union, Old Post, Ancient Britain* and mail coaches along the same route. Passengers for Warwick and Leamington changed for the *Vittoria* light coach, departing at 9.30 a.m. In the evening, the equivalent coaches returned, bound for the London terminus at the Bull & Mouth Inn.

Everyone and everything crossing the bridge – with the exception of pedestrians – had to pay a toll, ranging from 1s 6d for a stagecoach drawn by the full team of six horses to 1d for a horse and rider. Oxen and other cattle were charged at 3d per score, but calves, swine and sheep cost 5d per score, so driving a herd of sheep across the bridge would have been an expensive business.

The toll system must have aroused resentment and threats. Anyone attempting to 'unlawfully or maliciously burn, blow up or pull down or destroy the said bridge' faced transportation for life. The toll house keeper, Mr Hopcroft, was ordered to produce a quarterly list, naming those who had been convicted. There is no evidence that he made anything other than a nil return. Anyone damaging his toll house could be fined a sum not exceeding £10 with costs. Before 1827 pedestrians faced the hazard of coaches and horses thundering across the bridge, but, in that year, a cast-iron footway manufactured by the Eagle Foundry in Birmingham was installed.

Whether Mr Keen recovered his considerable outlay on the toll concession is unknown. He was unlikely to have realised that the advent of the railway age would kill off the coaching trade. The first intimation of this came with the opening of the Stratford to Moreton tramway in 1826. Many of the goods – including volumes of coal – that had been conveyed across the bridge by carts (those with three horses were charged a toll of 1s, and those with less than three, 9d) were now conveyed along the new railroad. Although Stratford did not become a part of the national railway network until 1859, the opening of George Stephenson's London to Birmingham railway in 1838 effectively saw off the

London to Holyhead coaching service. Due to loss of traffic, the levying of tolls on Clopton Bridge ceased in 1839. The toll house was taken over by James Cox as part of his timber yard between the Clopton and Tramway bridges at an initial rental of £7 per year – later reduced to £5. After this the building became redundant and went into decline. In 1951 the bridge and the toll house were given Grade I listings, but this did nothing to arrest the building's deterioration. For the last thirty years it has been on English Heritage's list of significant buildings in danger. In 2001 it was sold by Warwickshire County Council to Stratford District Council for a token of £1. A grant of £27,500 was given to enable essential repairs. Numerous companies were approached about leasing the building but negotiations always fell through because of the cost of refurbishment, the limited access and the restrictive conditions imposed by the listing. Rescue is at hand, however: the Stratford Historic Buildings Trust has obtained funding to refurbish the old building and bring it back into practical use from the Heritage Lottery Fund and from Historic England. Office space will be provided and there will be an exhibition about the history of the toll house and of the industrial area that was once concentrated around the canal basins and the banks of the Avon.

2. The Firm That Made the Cooperage for 'About the Best Beer Brewed in England'

The man who became Stratford's most eminent Victorian first visited the town when he was nineteen in 1825, signing the visitor's book at Shakespeare's Birthplace as 'Citizen of the World'. His father, Richard Flower, a radical pamphleteer, agriculturalist and utopian, had helped found a utopian settlement in Illinois when Edward was twelve. The boy shared the rigours of life in the wilderness. The settlers pursued the practical implications of their radical and egalitarian views and participated in the Freedom Trail for runaway slaves, often clashing with the slave owners.

Edward found much in England to attract him, and decided to remain. Soon after marrying Selina Greaves of Barford in 1827, he settled in Stratford and went into the timber business with James Cox on the canal wharves behind the One Elm. Cox, like Flower, was a Nonconformist and a political radical. In 1832 he opened a ragged school for forty poor children in Sheep Street. After a magistrates' hearing in 1837 his goods were distrained when he refused to pay the obligatory church rate towards the restoration of Holy Trinity, a church where he did not worship.

In 1831 Flower decided to open his soon-to-be-famous brewery on Birmingham Road after receiving a legacy on his father's death. Although this meant that the partnership with Cox ceased, the two men continued to work closely together. Flower provided the beer, and Cox the cooperage. After struggling at first, Flower thrived, epitomising the truth of Dr Johnson's dictum that his chosen trade could make a man as rich as Croesus.

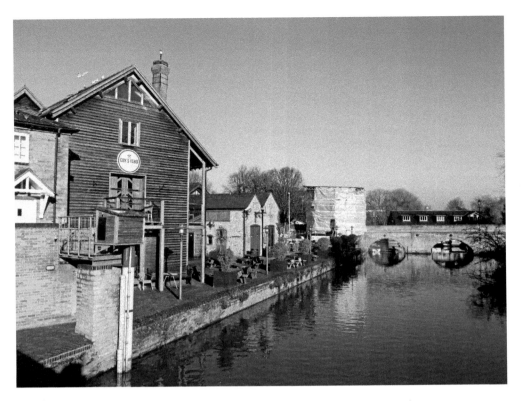

Above: Cox's Yard.

Left: Edward Flower.

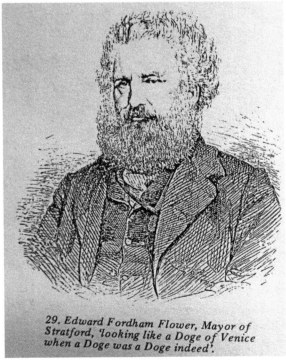

29. *Edward Fordham Flower, Mayor of Stratford, 'looking like a Doge of Venice when a Doge was a Doge indeed'.*

Technical innovations (Flowers was the first brewery to introduce coolers) helped produce what *Punch* described as 'about the best beer brewed in England'. James Cox was part of this movement towards wealth. In 1839 he moved his timber yard to Avon Bridge Wharf. This was an ideal site from which to run a business, adjacent as it was to the canal and the navigable river and the town's main thoroughfare.

The area around the canal basins (there were two then) became an industrial suburb with warehouses and workshops alongside the waterways. Among other activities, limekilns and fellmongers were established. The only surviving building from this era is the large warehouse that Cox built soon after his move to the wharf – naturally, it is constructed of timber. In the 1960s and '70s it was frequently described as an eyesore, together with its chimney stack, and there were regular demands for its demolition. It was saved in 1988 when it was given Grade II listing, with Historic England citing the fact that 'the building is an unusual survival and important as a reminder of the industrial nature of the area'. This is underlined by the fact that its builder and his business are still recorded in white paint on two sides of the edifice. In 1998 the building was given a new lease of life when it became a gastropub with a small working theatre. For four years it had the absurd name of The Silly Cow, but now it's back to its proper name, Cox's Yard.

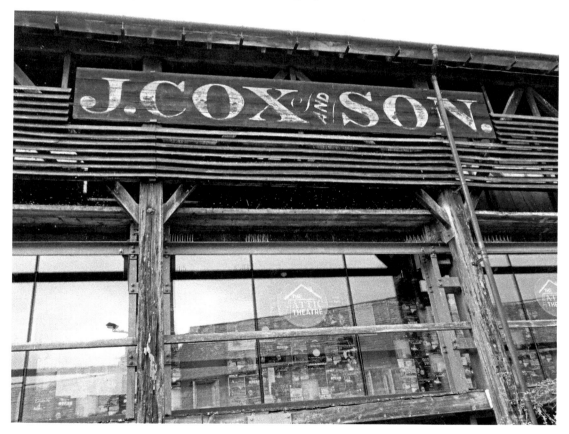

J. Cox & Son.

3. The Earliest Surviving Railway Truck

William James of Henley-in-Arden possessed creative energy and entrepreneurial vision on a grand scale. He made and lost the first great fortune of the railway age. After qualifying as a solicitor, he set up in practice as a land agent and handled a number of estates, including those of the Earl of Warwick and the Archbishop of Canterbury. He was engaged to complete the Stratford-upon-Avon Canal, which finally opened on 24 June 1816 – it had been a long time in the making. In 1820 he was worth £150,000, with an annual income of £10,000. In that year he launched a grand new enterprise: to build a 'Central Junction Railway' to link Stratford's waterway system – the River Avon and the canal – with London. This was six years before the opening of the Stockton and Darlington line. Thomas Telford was engaged as the consulting engineer and estimated that the first stage of line to Moreton-in-Marsh would cost £45,000. The engineer George Stephenson advised James to use the revolutionary new power of steam, but the uncertainties of the iron horse were rejected in favour of the more familiar flesh and blood variety. £35,500 was raised and an Act of Parliament obtained. Meanwhile, James had become obsessed with the potential of rail transportation, surveying a number of potential lines, including Liverpool and Manchester, largely at his own expense. Like so many of the entrepreneurs of the age, he was driven to bankruptcy. 'His fluency of conversation I never heard equalled', opined the great engineer, Robert Stephenson, 'but he was no thinker at all in the practical side of the work he had taken up.'

Despite the financial collapse of its architect, the tramway scheme proceeded apace. It opened amid great celebrations on 5 September 1826. At 10 a.m. a band set out from Stratford, preceding a party of dignitaries in five covered carriages. They were followed by the vital commodities of coal and lime in twenty-one trucks. 'Universal admiration and surprise were excited and warmly expressed by the spectators on seeing three fine horses … drawing a weight exceeding 15 tons, in four coal-loaded wagons along the line, even where there was the steepest ascent, without the least apparent extra-ordinary exertion.'

The *Warwick Advertiser* expressed the hope that the railway might 'prove a blessing to the poor … as affording the means of their being supplied with fuel, as well as many other necessaries of life, at a much cheaper rate than they hitherto could be afforded'.

The theme was taken up by a local poet:

> To see our iron railway, we are quite content.
> For what we've saved on firing will surely pay the rent.

A new trade made its mark in the local records when 'Thomas Lark, the driver of a Rail Road wagon' was charged with assault. The world's first recorded railway fatality occurred in Alderminster on 21 May 1830 when a child was run over.

The 16-mile track had cost the enormous sum of £80,000. In the first ten months of operation the receipts totalled £2,190, rather than the annual £3,000 required to break even. Nevertheless the tramway played a considerable role in the trade of the area for three decades, conveying 15,000 tons of coal annually by 1845. A branch line to Shipston-on-Stour was opened in 1845, but the grand design of a link to London was never fulfilled. In 1847 the tramway was taken over by the Oxford, Worcester & Wolverhampton Railway, which, six years later, opened Stratford's first primitive passenger service in adapted trucks, which conveyed the moderately reckless to mainline connections at Moreton. An account of this odd journey appeared in *London Society* in 1864:

> Attached to the carriage in front was a platform, on which the sagacious horse leaped to prevent being tripped up as we descended at a rattling good speed. The inspectors of the Board of Trade not having found this tramway, the occurrence, or non-occurrence of accidents was left chiefly to the goodness of Providence.

The guard applied his brake down inclines 'as tightly as he could; we all to the best of our individual capacities held on to our seats, and … thus managed to avoid being

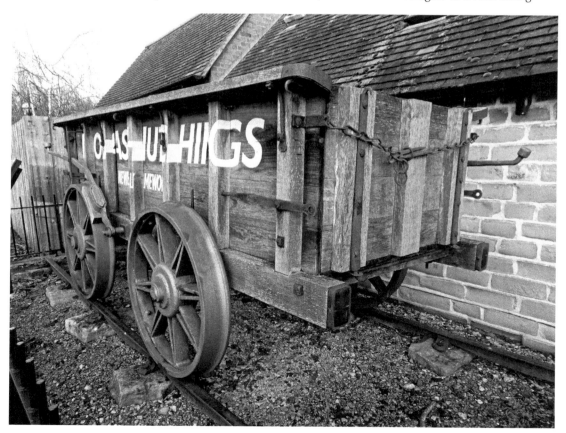

Tramway waggon.

pitched off head-foremost. When the carriage came to a standstill, the horse dismounted and drew us along as before.' On approaching a tunnel, 'the driver was kind enough to suggest that passengers should duck their heads as low as possible, and carry their hats in their hands'. The Royal Society for the Prevention of Cruelty to Animals took a less frivolous view of life on the tramway, bringing an action against the horse contractor, Joseph Haynes, for cruelly ill-treating and torturing his animals. He was fined the huge sum of £20.

The advent of steam ensured that the enterprise became a 'superseded idea', but, against all the odds, the tramway continued in service until the 1880s. The tracks were lifted in 1918 to be melted down as part of the war effort.

It is still possible to trace much of the tramway's route between Stratford and Moreton. Of course the most impressive survival is the graceful seven-arched brick bridge over which the carriages passed on the first stage of their journey to Moreton. Beyond that it is possible to walk for a mile or so along the embankment of the old railway, passing the pub on the left that bears the name of 'The Old Tramway Inn'.

A unique artefact can be seen on the approach to the bridge: the only surviving waggon from the tramway. Constructed around 1840, it belonged to Thomas Hutchings, a coal merchant of Shipston-on-Stour. After the tramway closed it was used as a chicken coop by an Alderminster farmer. The waggon was restored several decades ago, and placed on the last remaining short strip of flanged rail at Bridgefoot. It is still possible to see the blocks of stone, set between the rails over which the horse would have negotiated its way to Moreton.

4. The Statue Inspired by the Divine Sarah

Of all the monuments that exist to William Shakespeare, the most imposing stands in the Bancroft Gardens. The Gower Memorial is named after its creator, Lord Ronald Charles Sutherland-Leveson Gower, the youngest son of the 2nd Duke of Sutherland, who was a man of many talents. He was Liberal MP for the family seat of Sutherland between 1867 and 1874, but never spoke in the House. He was a trustee of the National Portrait Gallery and published works on the arts, biography and history, but his main interest was in sculpture, so he handed his safe Parliamentary seat to his nephew at the general election of 1874 and moved to Paris to join the workshop where Auguste Rodin had once been an apprentice. He soon set up his own studio with the noted Italian sculptor Luca Madrassi as his assistant.

Gower had been involved in the Shakespeare Birthplace Trust and in Charles Flower's project to build the Shakespeare Memorial Theatre. Through this connection he conceived the idea of designing a statue of Shakespeare as part of the theatre complex. His vision was on a grand scale. The statue of the poet aloft on a large pedestal would be surrounded on each corner by statues of characters from the plays: Hamlet representing philosophy,

Prince Hal representing history, Falstaff representing comedy, and Lady Macbeth representing tragedy.

According to *The English Illustrated Magazine* in 1895, Gower 'has known everyone worth knowing, from Garibaldi and Longfellow to the Empress Eugenie'. He was a friend of the artist John Everett Millais, who painted his portrait, and Oscar Wilde, whose homosexual proclivities he shared. The character of the foppish aristocrat Lord Henry Wotton in *The Picture of Dorian Gray* is probably at least partially based on Gower. Less happy was his relationship with the Prince of Wales, who wrote him a letter accusing him of unnatural practices, to which he wrote an angry riposte.

Another acquaintance was Sarah Bernhardt, the most celebrated actress of her day and herself a talented sculptress. Such was her dominance of the stage that she was lionised as *La Sarah Divine*. She paid a visit to Gower's studio to see the work in progress and showed particular interest in the statue of Lady Macbeth. There are two accounts of what happened next. One says that she suggested the drapes on Lady Macbeth's dress,[1] the other that she demonstrated precisely how Lady Macbeth should wring her hands, so the hands on the statue are modelled on hers.[2] Perhaps she did both. Gower sculpted the figures in clay before forming the casts in plaster. They were exhibited in Paris in 1881 before being cast into bronze at three different specialist foundries. The statues were shipped to Stratford and the monument was erected in the Theatre Gardens, with the figure of Shakespeare facing Holy Trinity Church. The monument was unveiled on 10 October 1888 by Gower's friend and probable former lover, Oscar Wilde. After this Gower ceased to be active in the artistic sphere, but devoted his life to a homoerotic form of hedonism. Unlike his friend Oscar, who was reckless in his disregard of the moral norms, he was adept at avoiding popular censure, although he had some involvement in the Cleveland Street scandal of 1889 when members of Lord Salisbury's administration were accused of organising a cover-up to protect members of the establishment who were clients of a male brothel. In 1898 he adopted his lover, a twenty-five-year-old journalist, Frank Hird, as his son. They remained together until Gower's death in 1916.

Sarah Bernhardt was to see the statue that she had helped inspire. In June 1899 she came to the theatre to play her famed version of Hamlet in French prose, supported by the Benson Company, speaking in English. It sold out weeks before the performance amid great excitement. Crowds gathered at the station to greet her. When the special train arrived, the flamboyant bestselling novelist Marie Corelli, who had recently moved to Stratford, greeted Madame Bernhardt in French, bestowing on her a magnificent bouquet, tied with the tricoloured ribbons of the two nations. 'The Divine Sarah' would recall this pilgrimage as one of her 'heart's memories'.

The monument survived unscathed after the fire that destroyed much of the theatre in 1926. When it was rebuilt the main entrance was no longer by the Theatre Gardens, so the Gower Memorial was moved to its present site on the Bancroft. In the process the figures were moved away from Shakespeare's plinth to follow its angles rather than its sides, so the whole creation lacks the effect the artist intended, but it represents an impressive first view of Stratford to the visitor.

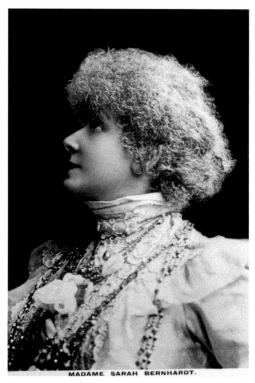

MADAME SARAH BERNHARDT.

Left: Sarah Bernhardt.

Below: The Lady Macbeth Gower memorial.

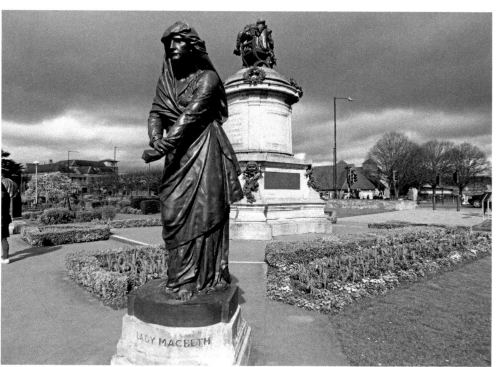

LADY MACBETH

5. The Sculpture That Never Made It to the Houses of Parliament

On 18 October 1834 what Guy Fawkes had failed to do was achieved by two workmen burning waste materials on a stove in the cellars of the House of Lords. The medieval Houses of Parliament were destroyed by fire.

A competition to design a new building attracted ninety-seven entries. It was won by Charles Barry, who was mainly known for his work for the Church Building Commissioners. He was assisted in the project by the most celebrated of Victorian architects, Augustus Welby Pugin. A competition was held to select works of art to adorn the new Palace of Westminster. Among the entries was *Hermaphroditus*, a sculpture by John Henry Foley, a twenty-six-year-old Irishman. The subject was a curious one to adorn a Parliament

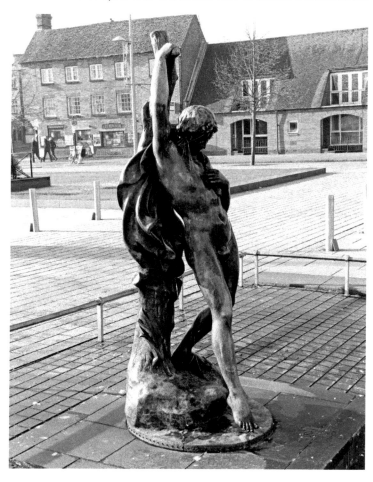

Hermaphroditus.

building. The story of Hermaphroditus comes from Greek mythology. He was a beautiful youth whose name was a compound of those of his parents – Hermes and Aphrodite. A water nymph named Samacis fell desperately in love with him and prayed to the Gods that they might be united for ever. They were, but not in the way she intended; their two bodies were merged into one androgynous form.

John Henry Foley became noteworthy in the very year of the competition when his sculpture, *Youth at a Stream*, was exhibited at the Royal Academy. The magazine, *Art Union*, considered it the most beautiful work in the exhibition. It may have been this enthusiasm that encouraged Foley to submit *Hermaphroditus* for potential inclusion at the new Palace of Westminster. It was unlikely, however, that parliamentarians would have taken kindly to the presence of a hermaphrodite in their midst and perceived the whole business as a satirical gesture at their expense, although Foley's work did eventually get into Parliament. He was commissioned to create marble statues of two seventeenth-century statesmen: John Hampden (1847) and John Selden (1854). Finally, his statue of Sir Charles Barry, the architect of the iconic building, was unveiled in 1866.

Foley created some familiar public sculptures, although most people would not know his name. The best known is the bronze statue of the Prince Consort on the Albert Memorial. He also created 'Asia', one of the four groups representing the continents that stand in each corner of the monument. His works are well represented in his native Dublin, including the statues of Daniel O'Connell in O'Connell Street and of Oliver Goldsmith and Henry Gratton on College Green. In Cork he created the statue of the temperance campaigner Father Matthew, with an outstretched arm pointing at the door of the public house across the square. He even produced a statue of the Southern hero Stonewall Jackson, which stands in Richmond, Virginia.

Although *Hermaphroditus* failed to make it into Parliament, it did feature in the Great Exhibition of 1851. The bronze cast was made by John Ayres Hatfield in his workshop in London (the firm is still in existence). Eventually, it was acquired by a dealer in fine art, Alfred Bullard, whose brother, Willie Porter Bullard, was mayor of Stratford between 1924 and 1926. They were probably related to the well-known local family of auctioneers with the same name.

On 11 October 1932 Alfred Bullard presented the statue to Stratford Borough Council. It stands on an arm of the canal basin in the Bancroft Gardens.

6. The Royal Shakespeare Theatre

The Art Deco Box Office

On 26 March 1926 a fire destroyed much of the Shakespeare Memorial Theatre. For the next five years the annual Shakespeare Festival was held in the town's Picture House. In 1927 a competition to design a new theatre was won by the only female entrant, Elizabeth Gilbert Scott. She was a member of a famous architectural dynasty but, at twenty-nine,

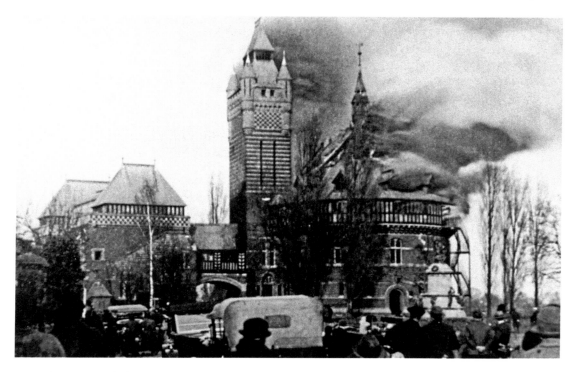

The Memorial Theatre fire, 1926.

her portfolio was slim. The *Stratford-upon-Avon Herald* was surely right when it described the decision as 'one of the first signal successes ever obtained by a woman in the realm of architecture.'

The press was almost unanimous in its praise. 'Miss Scott's plan is the only one that shows any theatrical sense', pronounced George Bernard Shaw, although he later said it looked like a fort on the Nile. The Stratfordians were equally inventive, calling the building 'a water tank', 'the new Soviet barracks' and 'a blot on the landscape'.

The new Shakespeare Memorial Theatre was one of the most impressive buildings ever built in the art deco style. Its clean-cut lines earned it the local sobriquet of 'The Jam Factory', but it was its internal arrangements that were the most impressive. Its beautiful teak airy foyer contained the classic art deco metal box office. A discreet passage led to an exquisite fountain court constructed of cloudy green marble: a lovely curved staircase of the same material led up to the circle foyer. Marvellous marquetry doors depicted the tools of the craftsmen who had created the 1932 theatre. The theatre had its limitations as a performance space, however. It was of its era and reflected something of the contemporary style of cinema. It was described as an architect's rather than an actor's theatre. The actor Baliol Holloway complained about the 'immense distance' between the stage and the front row of the stalls, which inhibited contact between actor and audience. Actors had been heard to say that it was like acting on the beach at Dover with the audience in Calais. To such criticisms, Elizabeth Scott responded that her intention had been to enable the incorporation of a platform stage.

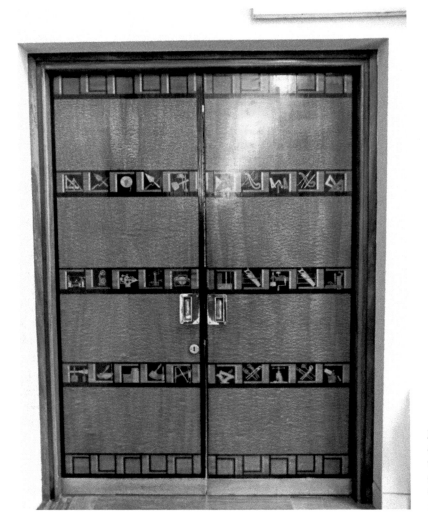

Marquetry doors depict the tools of the craftsmen who created the 1932 theatre.

Despite these criticisms, it has to be said that there were productions at Scott's theatre that will endure in the memory. Ones that spring to mind include Dorothy Tutin's Viola, Lawrence Olivier's Coriolanus with Edith Evans' Volumnia, Vanessa Redgrave's Rosalind, Donald Sindon's Othello, Peggy Ashcroft's all-day performance in *The Wars of the Roses*, the Lears of Paul Schofield and Robert Stephens and Stephens' Falstaff, Peter Brook's *Dream*, the *Much Ado* of Derek Jacobi and Sinead Cusack, Kenneth Branagh's Hamlet – everyone can make their own list.

The apron stage that Elizabeth intended was added in the 1960s and the performance space extended beyond the proscenium arch. This did not satisfy the theatre's critics. In the late 1990s a storm broke out when the RSC director, Adrian Noble, unveiled a scheme to demolish the whole building and build a 'Theatre Village' on the site. A local group styling itself 'Save our Jam Factory' was formed. The once-derided building had become an icon. Dame Judy Dench, doyenne of the RSC, joined the protest. The Twentieth Century Society

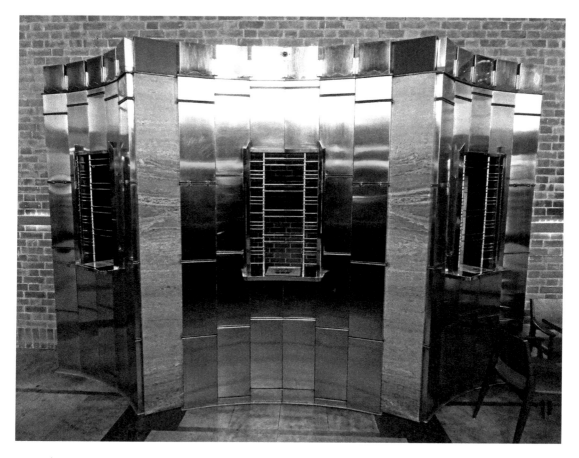

The RSC's original box office.

declared it would be an outrage if the first significant building designed by a woman was demolished. English Heritage pronounced against the demolition, but suggested that 'imaginative remodelling' might be the way forward. The RSC took the opportunity to get off the hook of public disapprobation and mounting costs, commissioning the architectural practice of Bennetts Associates to rework the existing building in a way that would preserve as much of the outstanding features of Elizabeth Scott's design as possible while creating a more appropriate performance space. The theatre was closed for three years while the desired result was achieved. The auditorium was gutted and a theatre-in-the-round, with an apron stage jutting into the audience, constructed. The distance from the stage to the furthest seat was reduced from 89 feet, which it had been in the old auditorium, to 49 feet. The new auditorium was generally greeted enthusiastically, although there must be those who miss the buzz of excitement that the previous one purveyed with all its memories. Nostalgia might also be felt for the riverfront verandas that gave the building the appearance of a Mississippi river boat when lit up at night. The verdict has been generally good, but surely no one can admire the completely anachronous observation tower that has been erected beside the building.

One of the great plusses of Bennetts' scheme is that the majority of Elizabeth's Scott's features outside the auditorium have been saved: the beautiful fountain court, the marble staircase and the artisans' doors. The lovely foyer has been turned into a bar with the art deco box office as the *piece de resistance*. When the bar is busy, the box office is hoisted upwards on its own traction system to create more space so that it sits serenely over the proceedings.

The Performance That Put the Theatre on the Map

Above the entrance to what is now the Swan Theatre are three terracotta friezes. They recall an event that was to put the Shakespeare Memorial Theatre on the world stage. In 1872 the wealthy local brewer Charles Flower embarked on a very ambitious project: to build a theatre in the town in honour of its most famous son. He selected the 2-acre site on the Bancroft, a little upstream from his home at Avonbank, as the ideal site. It was where Garrick's Jubilee Rotunda had once stood. The land was owned by Holy Trinity Church, but, in April 1874, the vestry authorised its conveyance 'for the purpose of building a theatre'. Flower handed the site to the newly formed Shakespeare Memorial Association. A public subscription was opened to build a theatre complete with library, art gallery and, if possible, Charles Flower's dream of an acting school. Optimistically, but worthily, it was announced that any surplus would be used to assist poor and deserving members of the acting profession.

Charles Flower set a good example by giving £1,000, but the response was disappointing: only another £1,000 was raised outside Stratford. Nevertheless, it was decided to proceed. The commission was granted to the Westminster practice of Dodgshun and Unsworth. The proposed design was a bold one, not concealing the fly tower, but making it a conspicuous part of the building. The end result looked not

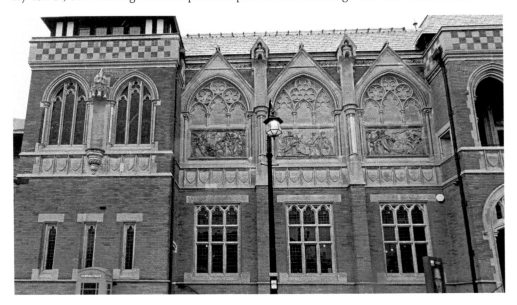

The Swan Theatre.

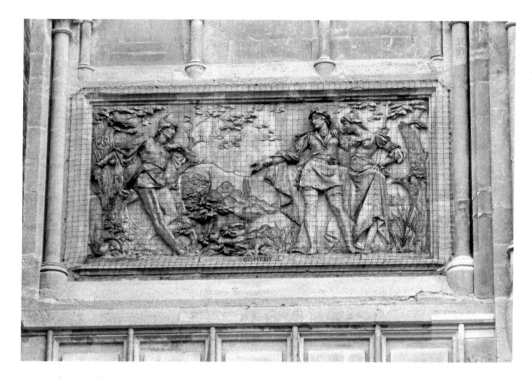

Swan Theatre detail.

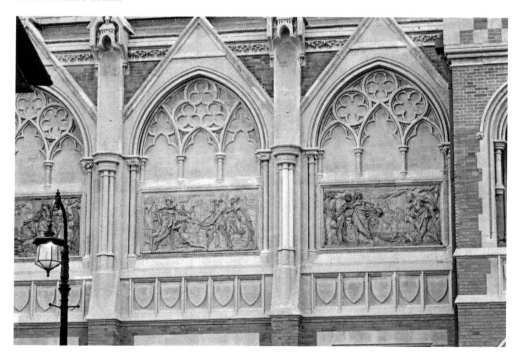

The Swan Theatre exterior.

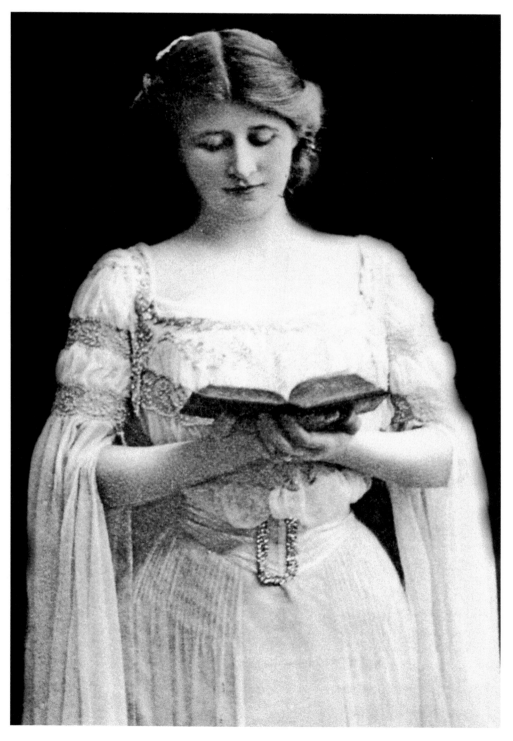

Mary Anderson.

unlike one of Ludwig II's castles, with curious turrets and gables, all faintly reminiscent in an odd Victorian way of Shakespeare's Globe Theatre.

Most of the London critics either treated the official opening on Shakespeare's birthday with derision or ignored it. One asked, 'Can it be imagined that the poet who sought in London the sphere for his intellectual life, stands in need of a Memorial which takes the shape of an addition to the list of petty provincial theatres?' Charles Flower replied in caustic terms: 'It is true that we are nobodies, but we have waited three hundred years for the somebodies to do something and they have not done it.' The theatre, at least, matched the taste of the age. Oscar Wilde regarded it as 'a beautiful building, one of the loveliest erected in England for many a long year'.

The opening production was *Much Ado About Nothing.* The veteran actress, Helen Faucit, star of the famous old Macready Company, was persuaded to come out of retirement at the age of sixty-seven to play Beatrice. Charles Flower's wife, Sarah, specially decorated her dressing room. This led to complications. Barry Sullivan, who played Benedick, said that unless he was given the same treatment he would walk out. 'You, my dear', said Charles Flower placidly to his wife, 'must send across some silver candlesticks, vases of flowers, and a nice lace pincushion for Mr Sullivan.' The Flowers must have wondered what they had let themselves in for. In the event, a capacity audience saw a performance that won general approval. 'Everything', wrote Helen Faucit, 'conspired to make the occasion happy.' It was a triumph for Charles Flower in his mayoral year.

After the opening triumph, the theatre did good business during the week-long annual festival around the time of Shakespeare's birthday. Apart from the occasional touring show, it was 'dark' for most of the rest of the year. The London critics appeared to have been right. The theatre appeared little more than a wealthy man's indulgence. That changed when the adulated young American actress, Mary Anderson, who had had two triumphant years on the London stage, expressed a desire to make her debut as Rosalind at Stratford before returning to America. Her Orlando was a future theatrical knight – Johnston Forbes Robertson. There was a scramble for tickets, despite prices being doubled. Every hotel was jammed. Her performance on 29 August 1885 received national critical acclaim. The theatre was on the map. Mary Anderson took no fee. The £150 raised by the benefit performance was used to commission two of the terracotta panels over the theatre's main entrance. One shows the gravedigger's scene from Hamlet and represents 'tragedy'. The second, representing 'comedy', shows Mary Anderson playing Rosalind. A third panel, denoting 'history' with a scene from *King John*, was commissioned by the architect of the theatre, W. F. Unsworth. All three panels were created by the German sculptor Paul Kummer.

Mary Anderson retired from the stage just five years after her triumph at Stratford. She married and went to live in Broadway, so she became a familiar figure in Stratford, even doing a few charity performances there during the First World War. She died in 1940.

7. The Windows Commemorating an Acting Company

From 1886 to the start of the First World War the same theatrical company participated in the annual Shakespeare Festival in Stratford's theatre. Under its charismatic leader, Frank Benson (later Sir Frank), the Company was a genuine fellowship. The Company became an institution and there was even an Old Bensonian Association, which held an annual dinner and produced a house journal, *The Flea*. The corporate spirit was fostered by sporting activities. It was said that Benson had once cabled his agent: 'Send me a fast bowler to play Laertes.'

Part of this heritage of solidarity is still with us. Despite the fact that it was a touring company endlessly navigating the provinces – the critic James Agate said that if a statue of

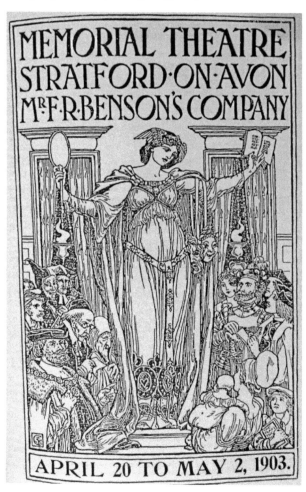

Programme from the Benson Company.

Benson were ever created, it should be on wheels – Stratford was its spiritual home. This is reflected in the fact that it became the custom for the Old Bensonians to present memorial windows to commemorate former colleagues who had died in the dress circle entrance to the old theatre. The actors are portrayed in the parts with which they were most associated. The first four were unveiled on May Day in 1905 in the Oriel window at the end of the picture gallery, along with a central panel depicting Shakespeare's coat of arms and the lines from *Henry V* that became the motto of the Bensonians: 'We few, we happy few, we band of brothers.' The windows were dedicated to the memory of T. J. ('Tommy') Merridew as Justice Shallow; Frank Rodney as a notable Buckingham and two members of the Company who had died in the Boer War, both in suitable martial roles; George Hippersley, who had died of enteric fever, as Henry V; and Alfred Ferrand, who was killed in action, as Hotspur. Perhaps it was the death of these young actors that inspired the Old Bensonians to create the windows.

Later that year another two windows were added, with Stuart Edgar portrayed as Sir Andrew Aguecheek and George F. Black as the Host of the Garter Inn from *The Merry Wives of Windsor*. Over the ensuing years, four more actors were commemorated. George R. Weir, a stalwart of the Company from its earliest days until his death in 1909, is portrayed as Bottom. In his obituary, the *Manchester Guardian* described him as 'a comic artist with a sense of poetry'. William Mollison appears as Cassius, and Edward A. Warburton as the Archbishop of Canterbury.

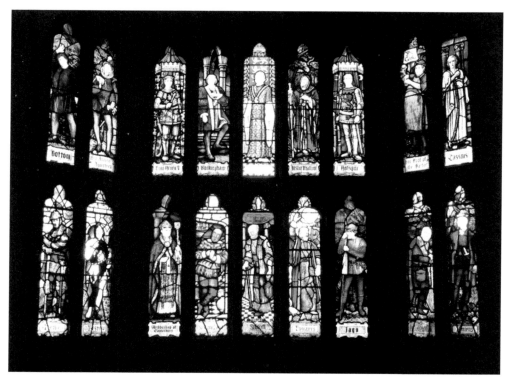

Benson Window at the RSC.

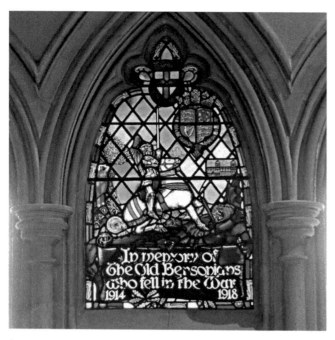

Benson Window at the RSC.

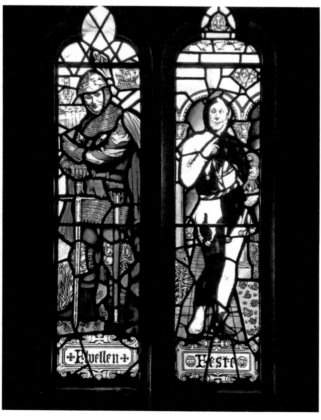

Benson Window at the RSC.

The fourth represents a deep personal tragedy. Lawrence Irving is portrayed as Iago. He was the younger son of the great actor, Sir Henry Irving. He spent three years in Russia in the diplomatic service, but the smell of the greasepaint was too strong and he joined the Benson Company in 1893. He was also a successful playwright. With his wife, the beautiful actress Mabel Hackney, he embarked on a tour of Australia and Canada in 1913, presenting four plays, including his own hugely-successful *Typhoon*. On 29 May 1914, the Irvings embarked at Quebec City aboard the Canadian Pacific liner *Empress of Ireland* to return to England. The ship collided with a Norwegian collier in the St Lawrence Estuary and sank rapidly. Lawrence Irving forsook a place of temporary safety to try to rescue his wife. Both perished in the icy waters, together with over 1,000 others. To Frank Benson, on tour in North America with the Stratford-upon-Avon Company, befell the task of identifying Lawrence Irving's body on the quayside at Quebec. Mabel Hackney's was never found.

The final frames in the Oriel window were unveiled in 1925 by Henry Ainley, a leading actor in Benson's Company and noted roué. They contain Alfred 'Uncle' Brydone, who joined the Company as early as 1889, portrayed as Adam, the good old man in *As You Like It*; A. E. George as Fluellen; Charles Bibby as Feste; Arthur Whitby as Sir Toby Belch; and John Glendinning, who had worked with Benson even before the Company was formed, appears as Shylock.

Scion of a noted Liverpool philanthropic family, Guy Rathbone appears as Amiens. He was a cousin of Frank Benson and elder brother of another prominent member of the Company, Basil Rathbone, who later achieved fame on the screen. Stephen Phillips was another cousin of Frank Benson, to whom he bore a strong resemblance, and of the poet Lawrence Binyon. The eldest of the precentor of Peterborough Cathedral's thirteen children, he was educated in Stratford at Trinity College. He turned down a place at Cambridge with the intention of sitting the Civil Service exams, but, in 1885, at the age of nineteen, he joined his cousin's newly formed theatre company. It may have helped that Benson regarded him as a 'first-class bowler of accurate length and varied pace'. He was with the Company for six years, rising to play a very young Prospero, the role in which he is portrayed in the window. His verse drama, *Paolo and Francesco,* based on an episode in Dante's *Inferno*, received rave notices, one critic describing him as 'the elder Dumas speaking with the voice of Milton'. Other plays followed. At the zenith of his career, he was earning huge money, but his hour of fame ceased and he resorted to heavy drinking and reclusive and, paradoxically, spendthrift behaviour. When he died in 1915 there was just £5 in his estate. His presence in the windows demonstrates that the Bensonians truly were a 'band of brothers' who never forgot a fellow.

In conjunction with the unveiling by Henry Ainlie, the doyenne of the stage, Dame Ellen Terry, unveiled a memorial window to the ten Bensonians who had perished in the First World War. It depicts St George slaying the dragon. The saint's face is that of Frank and Constance Benson's only son, Eric. Serving in the King's Royal Rifle Corps, he had been awarded the Military Cross and risen to become, at the age of twenty-nine, the youngest Lieutenant Colonel in the British Army. He discharged himself from hospital where he was being treated for an injured ankle and was fatally wounded while limping in front of his advancing battalion. His last words were: 'I don't mind.

I'm only sorry for my family. Give them my love.' At the very moment that Eric died, his father was to claim that he had appeared at his bedside and held a conversation with him. Despite being rejected for active service on grounds of his age (he was fifty-six at the outbreak of the war), he had managed to enlist in the French Red Cross as a stretcher-bearer.

Two of those previously commemorated appear in the memorial window – the comic actor Charles Bibby, and Guy Rathbone, who had risen to the rank of Major and won the Military Cross. Richard Conrick, a young Australian actor, perished when he rushed back to try to rescue someone from a blazing tank. Sergeant James Stanners was killed at the head of his men after the platoon officer had fallen. W. Ribton Haines had played Sir Toby Belch and Chatillon in *King John* in the Stratford season of 1909.

That the Bensonians were a true fellowship in death as well as life is demonstrated by the presence of three players of small parts: Frank Matthews, Arthur Curtis and Harold Chapin, whose sole appearances with the Benson Company occurred when he was seven years old. Born in Brooklyn, he was brought to England by his mother, the American actress Alice Chapin, who played Volumnia in *Coriolanus* in the season of 1893. The obvious choice to play her son, Marcius, was her own wee lad. He became an actor, appearing in John Galsworthy's noted play *Strife* at the Duke of York's Theatre, but it was as a rising radical dramatist that he was making his reputation. He wrote a number of well-received plays. They are rarely performed today, although his best-known work, *The New Morality*, was acted at the Finborough Theatre in London in 2005 and at New York's Mint Theater as recently as 2015. He married the exotically named actress Calypso Valetta and they had a son. When war came, he immediately signed up in the Royal Army Medical Corps, believing that the war might bring a new and more just order to Europe. He was killed on 26 September 1915 at the Battle of Loos. The presence of his name on the memorial demonstrates that even a seven year old was regarded as one of the 'Band of Brothers'.

The last two windows were dedicated in 1932, at the time of the rebuilding of the theatre following the fire of 1926, which the gallery survived. They were situated to the left of the original Oriel window. Frances Wetherall is portrayed as Emilia. She was a 'second' (understudy) to Constance Benson in several of her leading roles. She married a fellow Bensonian, Harry Reginald (H. R.) Hignett. E. Lyall ('Teddy') Swete is shown as Cardinal Wolsey. As well as being an actor, he was a director, writer and lyricist. Cissie Saumorez, portrayed as Lady Mortimer, was born Cissie Bartram in Bath. Presumably she adopted her exotic Hispanic surname to further her career as a singer, in which she achieved success with the D'Oyly Carte Company between 1889 and 1892, appearing in Gilbert and Sullivan's final operetta, *The Gondoliers*. With the break-up of that partnership, she toured America with *The Nautch Girl,* a fanciful operetta written by their successors at the Savoy Theatre, the composer Edward Solomon, and the lyricists George Dance and Frank Desprez. She joined the Benson Company in 1893 and appeared in over fifty roles, including those that utilised her talents as a soprano. In another Benson Company match, she married Arthur Whitby, who was commemorated in the Oriel window in 1925.

Leslie Faber is portrayed as the Earl of Westmoreland. He made his debut with the Benson Company and went on to achieve great success on the London and New York stages, and later as a star of silent films. He joined the army in the First World War and became a prisoner of war. It may have been this experience that precipitated his early death in 1930 at the age of just forty-nine. Sir Michael Redgrave said of him that he was 'so complete an artist that he could appear in two leading parts in the same play without the audience knowing it'.

It was not only actors who were commemorated. E. Garnet Holme joined the Company at the same time as his sister, Frances Wetherall, but soon graduated to become the 'Stage Master', as he is described in his window, which depicts him standing in front of the theatre. Christopher Wilson is the 'Music Master'. He composed 'Bolingbroke's March' for the Company's production of *Richard II*, which became the Bensonian anthem.

Janet Achurch spent just one season with the Benson Company and never played Stratford, but she participated in a fundamental moment in the theatre's development. During this one season she played Lady Macbeth, the part in which she is commemorated on the right-hand window. When the tour reached Leamington Spa, the performance was attended by Charles Flower, who was casting his eye over the company with a view to engaging it for the next festival season. It was a fiasco. One of many disasters occurred when she fainted and Benson, in carrying her off, banged her head on the set. 'Damn you, you clumsy fool', she shouted. 'You've broken my back.' Despite such setbacks, the Benson Company was duly engaged. If the incident was the reason that Janet Achurch never acted with Benson again, it affected her career not a jot. In 1889 she became one of the few Victorian actress-managers when she took over the running of London's Novelty Theatre, where she put on the English premier of Ibsen's *A Doll's House*, with herself in the lead. George Bernard Shaw, a great admirer, regarded her as 'the only tragic actress of genius we now possess', writing *Candida* with her in mind and only allowing it to be performed if she took the title role. She also played the female lead in his *Captain Brassbound's Conversion*. Despite such success, her life was blighted by tragedy. Her mother had died in giving birth to her. In 1889, while on tour in Egypt with her actor husband, she gave birth to a stillborn child, almost dying herself. The continuing pain led to her addiction to morphine and she died of morphine poisoning in 1916, aged fifty-two.

Alice Denvil was a noted performer of what was known as 'low comedy', playing parts like the nurse in *Romeo and Juliet* and Mistress Quickly, the role in which she is depicted in the window.

Otho Stuart made his debut at Stratford in the first Bensonian season of April 1886. He went on to play the gamut of leading Shakespearean parts, both with Benson and with his own company at London's Adelphi Theatre. The critic J. C. Trewin described him as 'one of the handsomest Oberons of all time'. He is depicted in that role on his window. It is reckoned that he played the part over a thousand times. A man of independent means, he spent a great deal of money subsidising the Benson Company and his own Adelphi ventures. The veteran actress Elinor Aickin was seventy-two when she joined the Company in 1906, so her appropriate nickname was 'Granny'. Equally appropriate was her casting as the nurse in *Romeo and Juliet*, the role in which she is portrayed here. Henry Jalland is portrayed as Horatio, a part he played to

Benson's Hamlet. In the early days of the Company, he combined his acting role with that of its business manager. Geneviève Ward was born in New York and became an opera singer in Italy under the stage name of Madame Ginevra Guerrabella. After her last role in *La Traviata* in 1862, she retired due to vocal difficulties and became an actress in England. She played with the Benson Company in her more mature years, being particularly noted for her fearsome performance as Volumnia, which may have led to her nickname in the Company as 'Old Ironsides'. It is in this role that she is portrayed in the window. In 1921 she became the first actress to be created a Dame of the British Empire.

Sir Frank Benson died on New Year's Eve in 1939 at the age of eighty-one. Eleven years later the central panel of the original window was removed to enable its replacement by one showing him as Richard II.[1] It was unveiled at a ceremony on 23 April 1950 by the Old Bensonians Dorothy Green and Balliol Holloway in the presence of many members of the profession, including Dame Sybil Thorndike, Sir Lewis Casson, John Gielgud and Anthony Quayle. Benson stood again at the heart of his Company.

8. The Theatre That Rose from the Dead

At 11 a.m. on Saturday 26 March 1926, little Eileen White, aged eight, was sent round the corner from her home in Sheep Street by her mother to run some errands for an old lady who lived on Waterside. 'There's a lot of smoke in the street', she told her. 'Oh, it's alright', replied the old lady. 'It's Mr Gisborne's bonfire'. It never occurred to her that the gardener on the Bancroft was unlikely to light a bonfire in springtime.

Late that morning a workman brought Alice Rainbow, the manager of the theatre, the startling news that a fire was raging on the stage behind the safety curtain. She went into the theatre and found it full of smoke. She reacted as many people probably would. To try to curb the fire she opened all the doors. This had the opposite effect and created a blazing inferno. By lunchtime, smoke was pouring from the roof. Fire brigades were summoned from miles around. The Warwick engine was still horse drawn and the horses were covered in foam as they came galloping down Waterside. The pumps were drawing water from the river and the hoses played on the flames, but it was a hopeless cause as the wind fanned the fire to greater intensity. Although the auditorium was engulfed, the wind was blowing the flames away from the Theatre Gallery, so a human chain was formed to carry the pictures across the street to the lecture room. Great crowds gathered to see the spectacle. They were not disappointed. The intense heat caused the tiles to fly off the roof and into the river. The art gallery was preserved intact, but the auditorium was gutted and the top of the tower disappeared completely. The Shakespeare Festival was due to begin in six weeks. The decision was taken to transfer it to the local Picture House, where it remained for five years. To her credit, the architect appointed for the rebuild, Elizabeth Scott, respected the old building and made it part of her plans for the new Shakespeare Memorial Theatre. The tower was demolished and the former auditorium reroofed and turned into first a rehearsal room, and later a conference centre. The occasional performance took place there, most memorably, in 1958, when Paul Robeson, the great American bass singer, gave a concert there. He was playing Othello in the theatre at the time.

Thanks to the generosity of an American donor in 1985, the Conference Centre was restored to its former glory as the Swan Theatre. The architect, Michael Reardon, was an intelligent choice. As consulting architect to both Birmingham and Hereford cathedrals, he was sensitive to the concept of preserving the historic quality of old buildings while making them live for a new era. This is exactly what he did here. A pointed slate roof with six garret windows evokes the Gothic spirit of the original. The auditorium seats 450 people in an intimate galleried setting, enhanced by the proximity of the audience to the apron stage. In terms of atmosphere, the Swan Theatre far exceeds that of its big sister next door. Those who consider it to be the finest theatrical space created in Britain since the war are probably right!

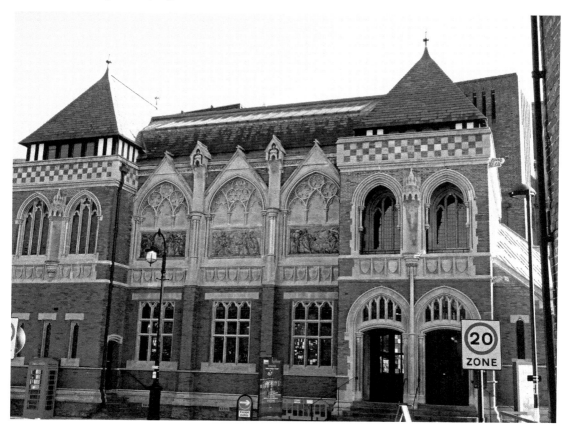

The Swan Theatre.

9. A Great Actress

In the Theatre Gardens there is a silver birch tree. At its base is a stone tablet bearing the inscription: 'A lass unparalleled'. The tree was planted in memory of the great actress Vivien Leigh, and the inscription adds her dates: 1913–67. The quotation is from *Antony and Cleopatra* and reads in full:

> *Now boast thee, death, in thy possession lies*
> *A lass unparallel'd. Downy windows, close;*
> *And golden Phoebus never be beheld*
> *Of eyes again so royal!*

Vivien Leigh appeared for just one season at Stratford. In 1955 she played Viola in *Twelfth Night*, Lady Macbeth, and Lavinia in *Titus Andronicus*. Her then-husband, Lawrence Olivier, played Malvolio and Macbeth and the title role in *Titus Andronicus*. They were the golden couple of show business. Vivien Leigh had starred in *Gone with the Wind*, the most successful film in box office history. No less than 400 actresses had auditioned for the part. She won an Oscar for her performance. She won a second Oscar in 1951 for her performance in *A Streetcar Named Desire*. Despite this rise to movie megastardom, she regarded the stage as her natural métier. 'When I come into a theatre,' she said, 'I get a sense of security. I love an audience. I love people and I act because I like trying to give pleasure to people.' In 1947 Lawrence Olivier had become the youngest actor to be awarded a knighthood. The couple had become both on- and off-set lovers while working on the film *Fire over England* in 1937. They had a considerable track record of performing in Shakespeare, both individually and together.

As may be expected, the appearance of the Oliviers created an unprecedented run on the box office. Over half a million applications were received for the 80,000 tickets available in the first tranche of booking.

Despite their golden image, this was not a happy time for the Oliviers. Vivien was suffering from the mental condition that is now defined as bipolar disorder, but of which there was then little more than a crude understanding. She suffered desperate depressions, which had worsened after she suffered a miscarriage in 1945. She was subject to recurrent bouts of the tuberculosis that eventually killed her and was given to bizarre sexual adventures. Word on the Stratford street indicated that, while playing the supposedly mute Lavinia, she had a penchant for mouthing obscene insults at Olivier in loud stage whispers.

John Gielgud, who directed the production of *Twelfth Night*, was highly critical of Vivien Leigh's approach to her part: 'She hardly dares at all and is terrified of overreaching her technique and doing anything that she has not killed the spontaneity of in over-practice.' Distinguished American directors took a kinder view of her. According to Elia Kazan, who directed her in *Streetcar*, she had 'the greatest determination to excel of any actress I've known'. Yet it was George Cukor, who had directed her in her other Oscar-winning role as Scarlett O'Hara, who probably came closest to the mark when he described her as 'a consummate actress hampered by beauty'.

10. Topal, Nick Bottom and the Owl

Stratford-upon-Avon contains a unique collection of lamp posts from around the world – some fifty of them in various parts of the town. They date from a time when such artefacts were individual to each place rather than being standard issue. Presumably they were

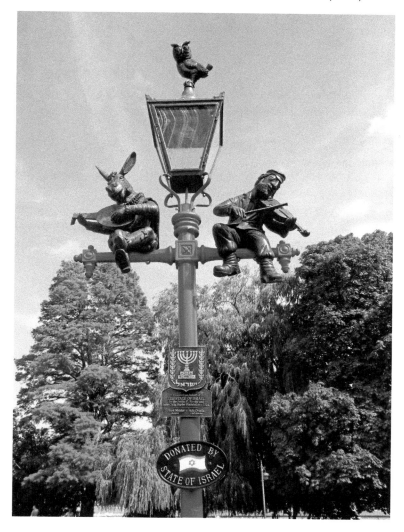

Topal lamp post.

presented to Stratford when they were uprooted to make way for the said standard issue. They really do constitute 'secret Stratford' though. There does not appear to be an obtainable comprehensive list of their sources and locations. Nor do they appear to feature on any website. The person who had the clever idea of starting such a collection remains anonymous.

One of the most striking lamp posts in the collection stands in Southern Lane, just outside the Theatre Gardens. It was presented to the town on behalf of the State of Israel by a Jewish foundation in America. As well as being a handsome lamp post, the edifice supports three incongruous but charming sculptures. On top of the structure sits the owl from Edward Lear's poem, 'The Owl and the Pussycat'. On one arm of the crosspiece sits Nick Bottom, the weaver turned into an ass, who for some reason is playing a mandolin. On the other part of the crosspiece sits the fiddler from *The Fiddler on the Roof*. The sculptor was Frank Meisler, who was born in Danzig in 1929 and educated in England.

11. The Pub Given its Name by a Theatrical Company

The Black Swan, universally known as the 'Dirty Duck', has been the world's most famous stage door pub for over a century. If anyone in Stratford were asked directions to a pub with the former name, the response would probably be a stupefied blink. The pub owes its name to the members of the Frank Benson's Theatrical Company, which had first performed an annual festival season at the theatre in the week around Shakespeare's birthday in 1886. It became customary to introduce a new play into the repertory each year. When the Bensonians returned for the festival of 1893, their leading man was suffering from typhoid that had been misdiagnosed as influenza. He was rushed to bed in a delirium and remained there for several weeks. It had been intended that the play to be performed on the birthday should be *Coriolanus*, but Benson's illness made this impossible. The governors of the theatre were loath to let a year go by without introducing a new play, so it was arranged that the Company should return to perform it in August. The weather was glorious. Many rehearsals were held in the theatre grounds or in the garden of the Black Swan – from that summer onwards, it was always referred to as the 'Dirty Duck'. The Bensonians were fond of giving nicknames to Stratford's hostelries. The Falcon was always 'the Canary' in their vocabulary.

The pub known by the Bensonians was smaller than the one we see today. This Grade II-listed building originally consisted of two townhouses dating from the seventeenth century. The central part of the building has been a pub since 1738 and was first recorded as the Black Swan in 1776. The building to the right became part of the pub in 1866, while the section to the left of the main entrance was incorporated in 1937.

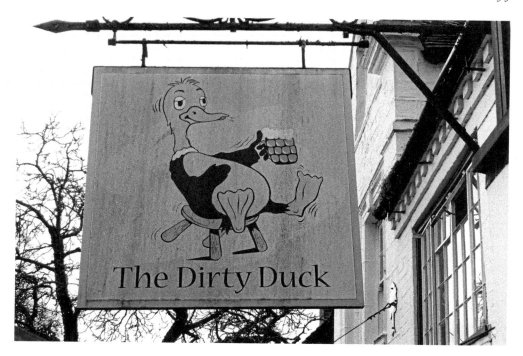

The Dirty Duck.

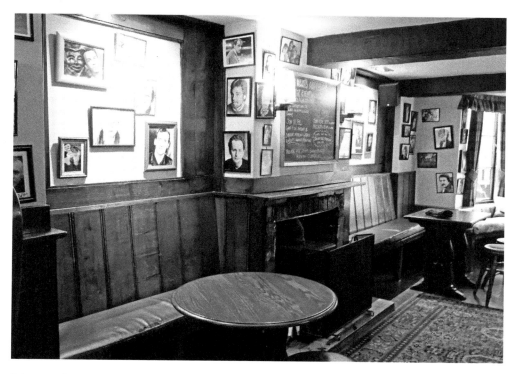

Dirty Duck interior.

The fact that the place is a celeb-watchers delight is personified in the many autographed photographs of actors that adorn the walls of the actors bar, many of them going back decades. Richard Burton, Lawrence Olivier and Judi Dench are all there, but it's a tribute to the democratic spirit of the profession that, to put it tactfully, less well-known actors also appear. It's worth noting that Kylie Minogue once pulled a pint there and Peter O'Toole broke the record for downing the Yard of Ale.

12. The Nine Men's Morris

On the corner of the Theatre Gardens nearest the chain ferry and opposite the Dirty Duck, a set of stone blocks are embedded in the turf. Most passers-by have no idea what they're there for. In fact it's a pitch for the playing of Nine Men's Morris, a very ancient game known to the Romans, and the Greeks before them. It reached a peak of popularity in medieval England. Boards have been found carved on cloister seats in Canterbury, Gloucester, Norwich and Salisbury cathedrals and at Westminster Abbey. 'The Nine Men's Morris is filled up with mud,' so says Titania in *A Midsummer Night's Dream*. This is a reference to the board game that was hugely popular in Elizabethan England.

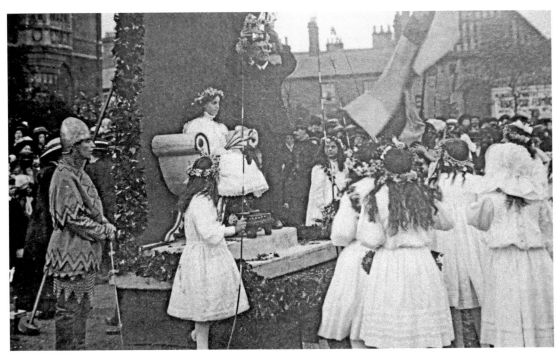

Benson crowning the May Queen.

The astonishing thing is that no one appears to know how this particular facility got there. It can't be all that ancient because the site contained osier beds for basketmaking until the late Victorian age, when the gardens were created. Most likely it dates from the period immediately before the First World War, when the actor-manager Frank Benson was seeking to awake 'the sleeping soul of England' by reviving traditional English folk culture. In 1907 he inaugurated a day of 'Old English Sports and Games'. Children danced around the maypole, skipped, sweated at the tug-of-war and a May Queen of dark eyes and raven locks was crowned. Later, the adults did their bit with catch-as-catch-can, pick-a-back wrestling, the greasy pole climbed for a leg of mutton, fencing, stick fighting and Morris dancing. On the river there was 'dongola' racing and tilting in boats, while an Elizabethan state barge, full of glee singers, rowed up and down.

So, what more likely occasion for the Nine Men's Morris to be created than for this wonderful day of old English sports and games?

13. Holy Trinity Church

Holy Trinity is one of the most beautiful and historic churches in the land. It is visited by thousands of people each year, most notably during the annual celebrations of

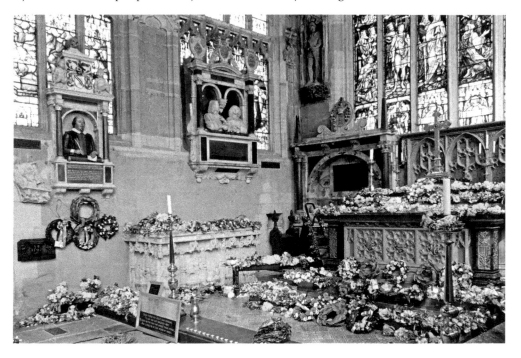

Holy Trinity chancel.

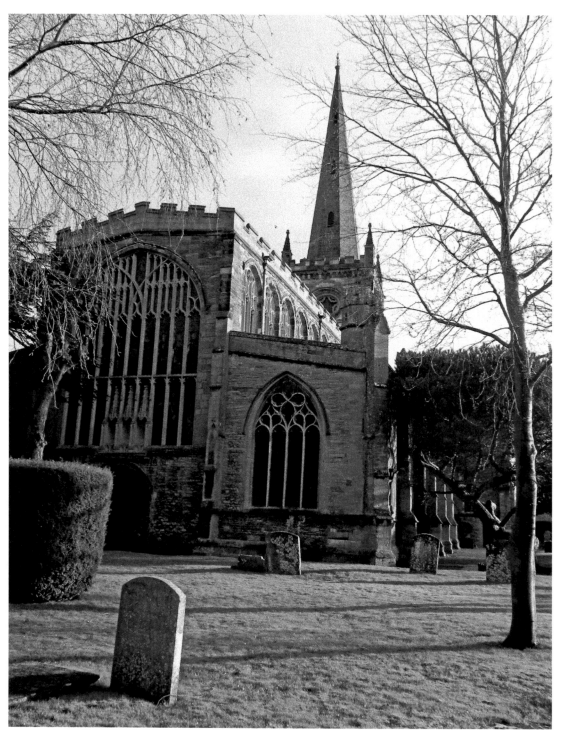

Holy Trinity Church.

Shakespeare's birthday, when flowers are laid on his grave. Many of the visitors miss the church's other wonders, some of which are described below.

The Sanctuary Knocker

Visitors to Holy Trinity enter through the two-storey north porch. The main west door is used only on ceremonial occasions. Entry to the nave is through massive oak doors, which were probably installed when the porch was built around 1495. Into the left-hand door is set another door, its smallness indicated by a cautionary warning to take care while passing through it. Set into this small door is a hooped ring, a sanctuary knocker. Any fugitive from justice that grasped it could claim sanctuary in the church for thirty-seven days. This right dated from Saxon times and was recognised throughout the land. This was due to the existence of dual legal systems – judicial and ecclesiastical – with different perspectives. The aim of the former was the punishment of wrongdoers and of the latter their penitence and atonement, so the ecclesiastical authorities were regarded as more lenient than their secular counterparts. It was the defence of these rights that was the basic cause of the martyrdom of Thomas Becket.[1] The only people who could not claim the right of sanctuary were witches, heretics, or those who had committed the crime of sacrilege against the church.

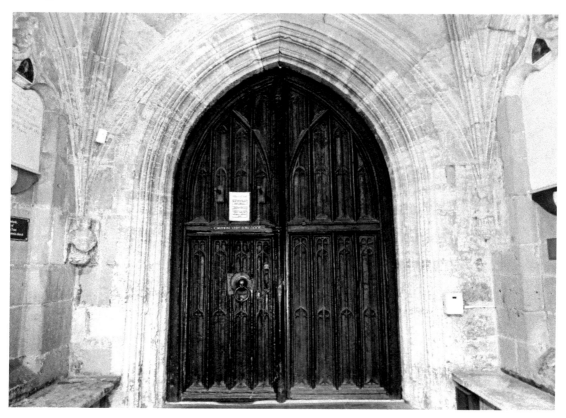

The sanctuary entrance.

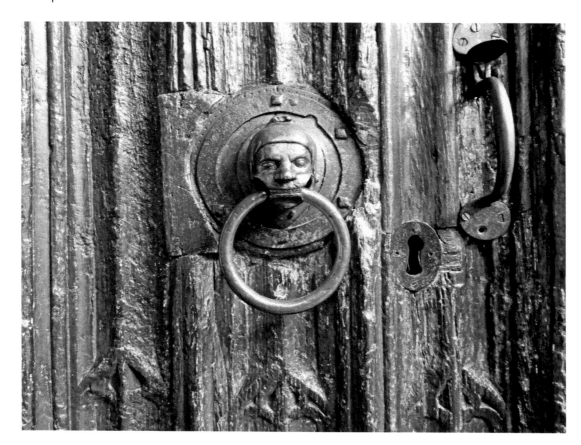

The sanctuary knocker.

During the period of sanctuary the fugitive was expected to be obedient and contrite, confessing his sins and discussing his case with the bishop or priest. At the end of this period the fugitive had to decide whether to stand trial or to plead guilty and 'abjure the realm' – a medieval form of banishment. An abjurer would have to depart from a designated port. This would often be some distance away. He would have to make the journey dressed in sackcloth and ashes, barefoot and carrying a cross. If he strayed from the main road, he would be executed on the spot. When he arrived at the port of embarkation, he was obliged to take the first ship that was sailing for his destination. If he had to wait for such a departure, he was to wade daily into the sea up to his midriff to symbolise his intention to leave these shores. A further hazard was that, in the course of his journey, the abjurer was an open target for his enemies. Given the odds against them, many abjurers may have decided it was better to take their chance in the forest with outlaws than to face the hazards of the open road and a place of exile with no means of support.

In fact the ring is a door handle as well as a knocker. It predates the door by some 200 years. Shakespeare would have known it. Indeed he refers to the right of sanctuary in *Richard III*, where the cardinal defends it as an honoured rite, but to no avail. The widowed queen, Elizabeth, has sought sanctuary in Westminster Abbey with her young son, the

Duke of York, to escape the evil intentions of Richard of Gloucester. Richard's ally, the Duke of Buckingham, then attempts to coerce the cardinal into refusing sanctuary to the child.

The right of sanctuary did not long outlast the lifetime of William Shakespeare. It was abolished in the reign of James I in 1623.

The Processional Cross in Memory of an Actor

One of the great moments of the old Memorial Theatre came in the festival of 1902. The doyenne of the stage, Ellen Terry, came to play Queen Katherine in *Henry VIII*, fulfilling a pledge she had made twenty years before – that one day she would act under Frank Benson's management. 'Those of us who can look over the vista of the years and note the swell of enthusiasm which greets our Shakespeare Festival', wrote a local theatre buff, 'will find it hard to recall one in which enthusiasm has been so wide and deep and real.' When Miss Terry went on stage, she received a prolonged standing ovation, but it was not she who would be most remembered on that amazing evening. It was public knowledge that Frank Rodney was suffering from cancer of the tongue. He was one of those solid actors who are the mainstay of any classical company. 'He was the best Clarence, Buckingham, Bolingbroke, Iago and Mercutio that T ever saw', wrote the noted critic James Agate. The shocked Benson, knowing he would never act again, even if he survived an operation in the following week, offered him any part in the repertory. He chose the part of Buckingham in this play. A deathly hush descended as he spoke his final terrible, majestic lines in Act Two.

> All good people
> Pray for me! I must now forsake ye: the last hour
> Of my long weary life is come upon me. Farewell.
> And when you would say something that is sad,
> Speak of how I fell. I have done and God forgive me!

On 8 May the *Stratford Herald* recorded that:

> The painful circumstances give a particular pathos to the Duke of Buckingham's fine speech. Mr Rodney delivered it with much feeling and with more than the usual emphasis … At the close of the scene he was called before the curtain and met with such a reception as he will probably never forget. The audience loudly cheered him and called him back three or four times.

At the curtain calls, he was shouted for again, but he did not return. He had taken his exit from the stage and, a few weeks later, from life itself.

Frank Benson also brought drama from the beginning of life into this production. Always a stickler for accurate effects, he engaged a baby from Waterside to play the tiny Princess Elizabeth. The infant screamed the house down and had to be taken off the stage.

A fine silver processional cross was given to Holy Trinity Church in memory of Frank Rodney as a result of a subscription raised from his colleagues and his family. The words of his final speech are engraved upon it. When it is not being carried in services, it can be seen in its wooden box by the choir stalls.

42

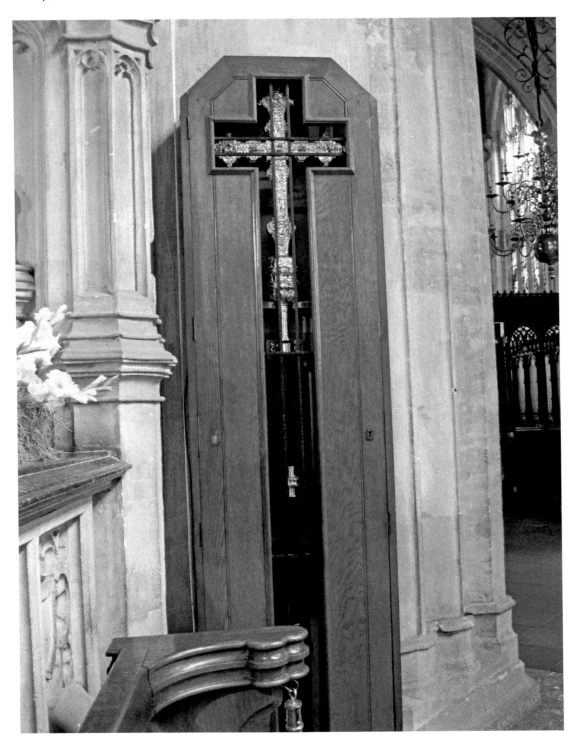

Frank Rodney Cross.

The Empty Tomb

Hugh Clopton was probably the greatest benefactor to Stratford in its history (although some might think the same of the Flower family). He was born around 1440 at nearby Clopton House where the family had lived since the reign of Henry III and from whence it took its name. As a younger son, he decided to make his fortune in London. Like Dick Whittington before him, he became a prominent member of the Mercer's Company, Lord Mayor of London and a knight of the realm. He amassed a huge fortune of £15,000 – over £4 billion in today's money. Like William Shakespeare, he never forgot his native place. Around 1483 he used some of his great wealth to build New Place, 'a praty house of brick and tybre' in Chapel Street, probably the town's first brick building, later to be the Stratford home of William Shakespeare. Sir Hugh rebuilt and beautified the Chapel of the Guild of the Holy Cross opposite his home.

Sir Hugh bequeathed 5 marks each as dowries to twenty maidens of 'good name and fame' living in Stratford, £100 to the town's poor householders, and £50 to rebuild the cross aisle at Holy Trinity. His greatest gift to Stratford was the 'great and sumptuous bridge upon the Avon'.

In his last will and testament, written just before his death, Sir Hugh gave instructions for his burial. He desired to be buried at night with modest ceremony and had his tomb built in his lifetime. In fact Sir Hugh died in his London home and was buried in the parish church of St Mary at Lothbury. His Stratford tomb remains empty.

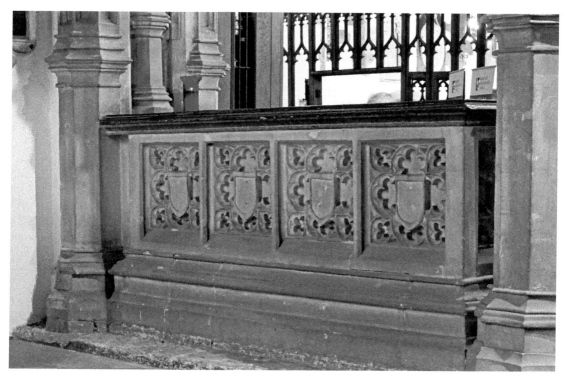

Hugh Clopton's empty tomb.

The Tomb of the Master of the Ordinance

It would appear that Sir Hugh Clopton never married. He may have regarded nuptial bliss as a diversion from the serious task of making lots of money – and, of course, giving a deal of it away to good causes. As such, his estate eventually passed to his elder brother's sixth-generation descendent, Joyce Clopton. In 1580 she married a West Countryman,

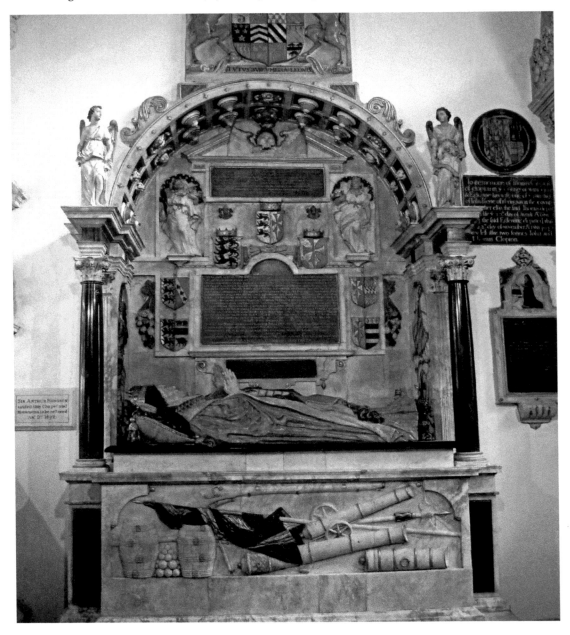

Cannons adorn the tomb of the Master of Ordinance.

George Carew, who like his friends Francis Drake and Walter Raleigh was a swashbuckling adventurer, voyaging with Sir Humphrey Gilbert and accompanying the Earl of Essex on his assaults on Cadiz and the Azores. He was also a thug, personally executing six Irish prisoners of war that he suspected of killing his brother at the Battle of Glenmalure (people do get killed in battles), for which he received a mere reprimand. He devastated vast tracts of Irish countryside. On his own confession, he commissioned the poisoning of the Irish hero Hugh O'Donnell, Lord of Tyconnel.

Carew held a number of offices of distinction: Ambassador to France, President of Munster, Member of Parliament, Governor of Guernsey and Treasurer to Queen Henrietta Maria. In recognition of his services, he was created Earl of Totnes in 1626. The position of which he was most proud – Lieutenant General of Ordnance – is shown on his tombstone with its carved cannons, gunpowder barrels, cannonballs and a flag lowered in mourning. The tomb is one of the finest of its period. The Earl and his Countess lie side by side, wearing their robes and coronets. A plaque of black marble shows a more human side of Carew, recording in Latin that the Countess was 'the most sorrowful widow of the dearest and most meritorious man'. A genealogy of heraldry was created, with the Carew and Clopton coats of arms individually depicted and then paired. Two shields on each side of the plaque depict past pairings of the Carew and Clopton dynasties, while surmounting all is a large shield divided into twelve, showing the extensive genealogical history of the Carew family.

The Earl's funeral helmet hangs on the wall to the left. On the right a small plaque commemorates the Countess's 'waiting gentlewoman', Amy Smith, who had expressed a desire to be laid to rest at her mistress's feet. In fact, she died in Surrey, but the Countess kept faith with her wish and brought her body back to Stratford to be buried near where she too would be laid to rest. The Earl and Countess had no surviving issue, but he had fathered an illegitimate son before his marriage. Sir Thomas Stafford had a distinguished career as a courtier, parliamentarian and historian of the Irish wars. At his death in 1655, he was buried in his father's tomb.

The Woman on Two Monuments

Joyce Clopton appears on two monuments in her family's chantry chapel: as a mature woman, a countess next to her husband, but also as the much younger woman of forty years before. Her effigy stands above the tomb of her parents, together with those of her six siblings: Elizabeth, Ludowicke, Margaret, William, Anne and another William. The first William had died in infancy and is portrayed in his swaddling clothes, as are Elizabeth and Ludowicke. Margaret died in childhood and is depicted as a young girl. The three who survived infancy and childhood are depicted as holding shields with armorial bearings. The second William is depicted as a youth and must have died soon after the tableau was created. He had been the sole direct male heir. The figures of Joyce and Margaret, the sole survivors to adulthood, are in contemporary costume with large ruffs.

The tomb of the parents is another splendid creation. The figure of William Clopton, grandson of his namesake who had inherited Hugh Clopton's fortune in 1496, is dressed in full armour, with his sword by his side. His lady wears a gown and fashionable ruff and the rare sight of a pomander on her chest.

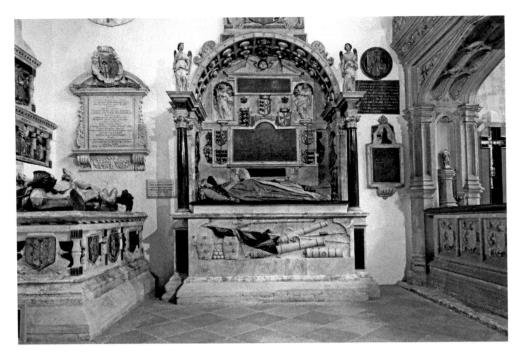

Clopton Chapel.

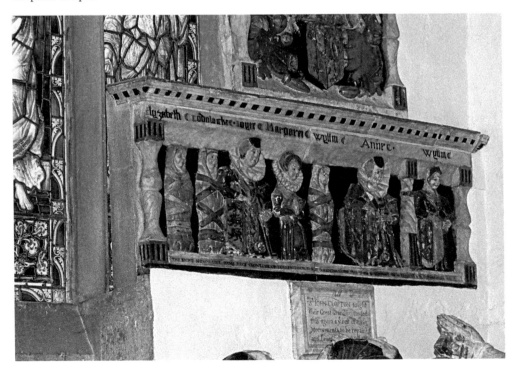

The effigies of the Clopton children.

The Controversial Pulpit

The novelist Marie Corelli was the greatest controversialist in Stratford's history. In 1899 she rented 'Hall's Croft' in Old Town near the church making 'Mason's Croft' in Church Street her permanent home two years later. Her interest in Stratford led to a genuine desire for its conservation. Her first campaign was a great success. When the poet, writer, translator and private secretary to Queen Victoria, Sir Theodore Martin, proposed to erect a large memorial to his wife – the actress Helen Faucit, who had died in 1898 – opposite Shakespeare's monument in Holy Trinity. She wrote a letter of protest to *The Morning Post* that engendered considerable support, but her triumph was due to assiduous research. When Sir Arthur Hodgson, the High Steward of the Borough, applied for a faculty to remove two monuments to make room for the memorial, she secured the opposition of the descendants of those commemorated. Thus baulked, Sir Theodore decided instead to donate the huge sum of £1,000 to erect a pulpit in his wife's memory and commissioned a design from the eminent Gothic Revival architect George Frederick Bodley, Holy Trinity's consulting architect. This ran into trouble from an equally determined source. The vicar,

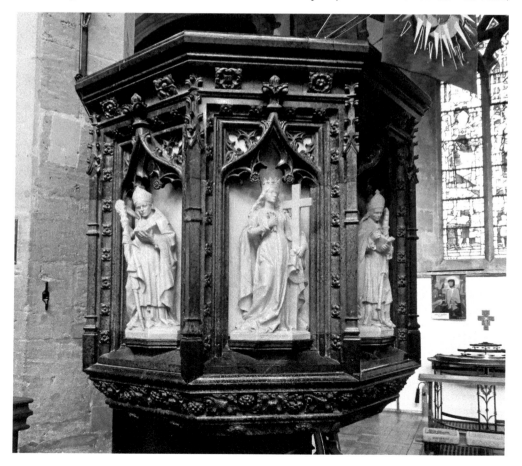

Helen Faucit as St Helena.

Revd George Arbuthnot, was a controversialist to rival Marie Corelli and he took against Sir Theodore's scheme, wanting the pulpit to be of carved oak rather than the stone of Bodley's design. With no protesting relatives in view, the faculty was granted. In disgust, the vicar boycotted the dedication service for the new pulpit.

The pulpit is surrounded by five figures of saints cast in alabaster. The central figure is Helen Faucit, depicted as Saint Helena holding the one true cross. The figure of Saint Jerome, translator of the *Vulgate*, aroused further controversy. The vicar protested that he was depicted wearing a cardinal's cap when he was not even a bishop, and took direct action by organising for the top of Jerome's crozier to be filed off. This led to a storm of protest, but the crozier remains without its crooked top to this day.

A Poem by Rudyard Kipling
In 1919 Rudyard Kipling published his 'Epitaphs of the War' in his anthology of poems, *The Years Between*. They were modelled on the epitaphs to be found in *The Greek Anthology*, which had been written over the centuries. Each contains a specific response to death. In the St Peter Chapel at Holy Trinity Church on a grey-marble tablet is his epitaph for the actors who had fallen in the First World War:

> We counterfeited once for your disport,
> Men's joy and sorrow, but our day has passed.
> We pray you pardon all where we fell short,
> Seeing we were your servants to this last.

The tablet was designed by the noted sculptor Sir George Frampton, whose best-known work includes the memorial to W. S. Gilbert on the Victoria Embankment, the Peter Pan sculpture in Kensington Gardens and the Edith Cavell memorial in St Martin's Place.

A Man of Sound Dealing
In his will, Alderman Richard Hill, a wool draper of Wood Street, left the useful sum of 10s to the vicar of Holy Trinity, John Bramhall, 'for a sermon at my buriall'. If the words on his tombstone are anything to go by, the vicar would have no difficulty in finding good things to say about him. It may well have been the vicar who composed the words in Hebrew, Latin and Greek. The inscription in Hebrew is a sentence from the Book of Common Prayer of 1552, which may have been read at Hill's burial service. 'Naked shall I return thither: the Lord gave and the Lord hath taken it: blessed be the name of the Lord.' (Job 1.21)

The verses in English appear to have been written by a member of Hill's household and are unstinted in their praise of him. They are somewhat eroded, but the original version appears to have read something like this:

> Heare borne heare lived heare died and buried heare
> Lieth Richard Hill thrise Bailiff of the Burrow
> Too matrons of good fame he married in Godes feare
> And now releast in ioi [joy] he reasts from worldlie sorrow
> A woolen draper beeing in his time

Whose virtues live whose fame doth flourish still
Though he disolved be to dust and lime
A mirror he and paterne mai be made
For such as shall succeed him in that Trade
He did not use to sweare to glose eather faigne
His brother to defraude in Bargaininge
He would not strive to get excessive gaine
In ani cloath or other kinde of tinge.
His servant I this truth dooth testifie
A witness that beheld it with mi eie.

Richard Hill was first elected bailiff of the borough in 1564 – the year William Shakespeare was born. As a local woollen draper he almost certainly did business with John Shakespeare, who was a dealer in wool. The poet's father was a beneficiary of that generosity of spirit described in the epitaph. Alderman Hill put up the bail after his brother Henry failed to repay a debt that John Shakespeare had guaranteed. The good alderman's intervention probably saves him from going to jail.

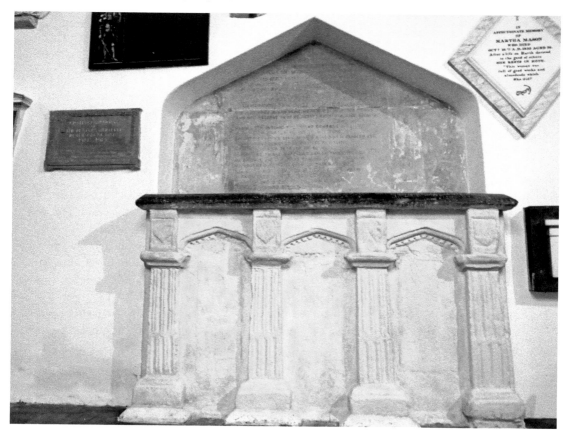

Epitaph to Richard Hill.

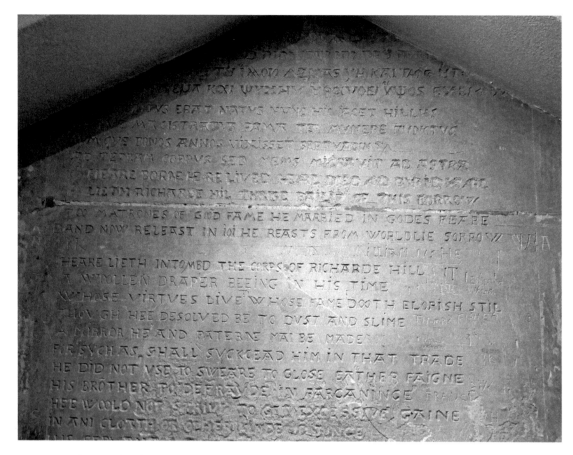

Epitaph to Richard Hill.

The Misericords

In the late fifteenth century the dean, Thomas Balsall, rebuilt the choir at Holy Trinity as the exquisite structure that survives to this day. The work reveals the skills of two very different master craftsmen. Their styles are contrasting, but they had one thing in common. Neither was familiar with contemporary trends in his craft. One created a delicate tracery throughout the choir, but in the Early English style of two centuries before, which he might have seen in the great cathedrals. The earthy creations of the other demonstrate the continuity of a peasant culture within the medieval Ecclesia. He carved the fantastical and bizarre misericords on the choir stalls. A misericord, or mercy seat, is a wooden image under a folding seat, intended to act as a partial support for those in the choirstalls during long periods of chanting the eight daily divine offices. Appropriately, the word derives from the Latin *misericordia* – 'to feel pity'.

Clearly sacred images were inappropriate as decorative effects on a platform intended to support the human rear end, so an entirely secular form of art evolved, although the armrests are decorated with images of angels, their eyes raised upwards in adoration. The misericords in Holy Trinity are among the finest anywhere. Miraculous they escaped

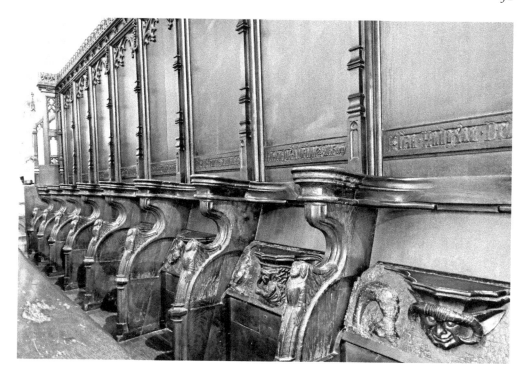

Misericords.

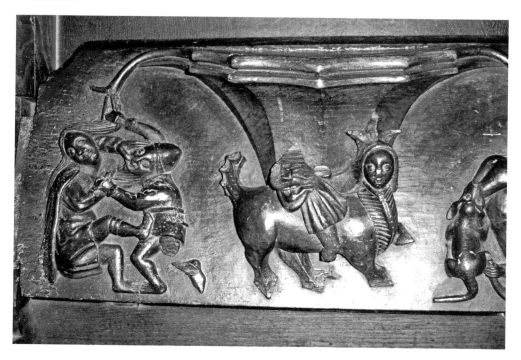

Detail of the misericords.

the destruction wrought by the Puritans in the seventeenth century. Maybe they just never thought to look under the seat.

The twenty-six carvings include such folk memories of the crusades as a wonderful Saracen's head and a sphinx with a rider. Also featured is an ostrich swallowing a horseshoe, a mermaid combing her hair with a hand mirror, and the explicit sexual symbolism of *luxuria* (lechery) is invoked as a naked woman rides a stag. Domestic discord is represented by a wife seizing her husband's beard and pummelling him with a frying pan, perhaps providing some consolation to the monks of the chapter for their vows of celibacy. Oddest of all is the depiction of two rampant bears, flanked by a chained ape, which provides a urine sample for another ape to examine.

The Tomb of John Combe

Although William Shakespeare made a lot of money, there was one man in Stratford whose wealth was probably greater than his. His house at New Place was the second largest in Stratford, only exceeded in size by The College, John Combe's mansion near the church.[2] Combe's wealth was based on lending money at interest and engaging in frequent legal actions against defaulters. Within four years of his death in 1614, an epitaph was published 'upon John Combe of Stratford-upon-Avon, a notable Usurer, fastened upon a Tombe that he has caused to be built in his lifetime'.

> Ten in the hundred here lies engraved,
> A hundred to ten his soul is not saved.
> If anyone asks who lies in this Tombe.
> 'O ho!' (quoth the Divell) 'tis my John a Combe.'

Similar verses on an unnamed usurer had been printed previously. In 1634 an army officer, Lieutenant Hammond, visited Holy Trinity. He claimed to have seen the verse attached to the tomb, recording that Shakespeare 'did merrily fann up the witty and facetious verses', but that pressure of time did not allow him to copy them. John Aubrey later added the detail that the poet had extemporised it in a tavern during Combe's lifetime. It was indeed common practice to make up mock epitaphs about people in their lifetimes and a number of these are attributed to William Shakespeare. Curious as it may seem, it appears that the verse was indeed affixed to the tomb. As late as 1673, one Robert Dobyns noted that 'since my being in Stratford, the heirs of Master Combe have caused these verses to be erased so that now they are not legible'.

In fact, it appears that Combe was more generous in death than the legacy for which his posthumous reputation gave him credit. He left the considerable sum of £20 to the poor of Stratford and also £5 to William Shakespeare, so if the quip was indeed written by the poet in his lifetime, he took it as the joke for which it was intended. In death, he did not lose the habit of usury, even putting it to the wider good. According to the inscription on the monument, he left £100 'to be lent unto 15 poore tradesmen of ye same burrough from 3 yeares to 3 yeares changing ye p[ar]ties every third yeare at ye rate of fiftie shillings p. anum ye w[h]ich increase he appointed to be distributed toward the reliefe of the almes peope theire.'

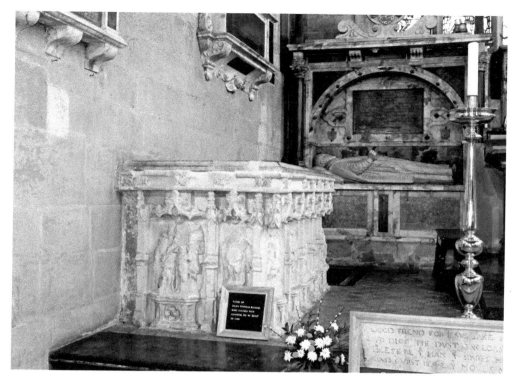

Combe and Balsall's tombs.

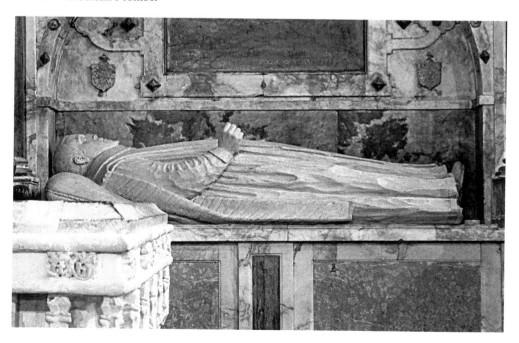

John Combe's missing foot.

Combe left the huge sum of £60 to create his monument. It was sculpted by Gerard Johnson, a young man of Flemish origin who worked near the Globe Theatre in London. It is likely that William Shakespeare commended him for the commission. Two years later he performed the same task for the poet.

The mystery deepens with the visit around 1618 of the poet and antiquary John Weever. He copied into his notebook a verse that he had seen on Combe's tomb that is somewhat different from the one attributed to Shakespeare:

> How ere hee livd judg not
> John Combes shall never bee forgor
> Whilst poore have memorie, for hee did gather
> To make the poore his issue, hee their father
> And record of his Tylth & Seedes
> Doth Crowne him in his later deedes.

It seems unlikely that, as Weever suggests, the purpose of John Combe's entire career in moneylending was to benefit the poor after his death. His posthumous generosity may have been in the hope of securing eternal salvation and the fifteen poor tradesmen representatives were from the very class that he had exploited in his lifetime.

Perhaps the second set of verses was a reaction against the first. It was certainly widely believed that it was William Shakespeare who wrote the verse mocking Combe the usurer. The Combe family was not the most popular in town. John's nephews, William and Thomas, caused stress and controversy in 1614 when they proposed to enclose the common fields at Welcombe, thereby evicting the smallholders who farmed there without compensation. The sad epitaph of William Combe's daughter, Judith, shows that the family had a human face. She was to marry her cousin, Richard Combe of Hemel Hempstead,

> Had not death prevented it by depriving her of her life, to the extream grief and sorrow of both their friends, but more especially of the said Richard Combe, who in testimony of his unfeigned love hath erected this monument for perpetuating her pious memory. She tooke her last leave of this life the 17th day of August 1649. In ye armes of him who most entirely loved her and was beloved of her even to ye very death.

Exquisite busts of the loving couple appear on their monument on the north wall of the chancel. They clasp hands and Richard presses his right hand against his heart. Her left hand rest upon a skull.

The story of John Combe has what might be described as a footnote – literally. As part of the eighteenth-century penchant for obtaining practical souvenirs of memorable visits, an unknown person stole the feet from his effigy. In 1894 the vicar received a letter from a gentleman who claimed to have the missing left foot. It proved a perfect fit. The right one is missing to this day.

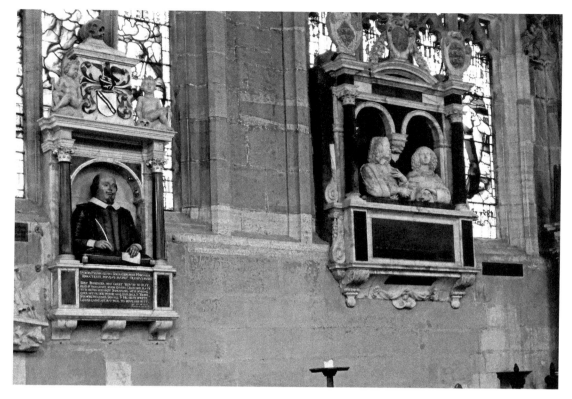

Shakespeare and the busts of Richard and Judith Combe.

The Epitaph That Proves Who Wrote Shakespeare's Works

In recent years harmless eccentrics have come up with every sort of preposterous theory as to who might have written the works that are adorned with the name of William Shakespeare. In recent years Edward De Vere, 17th Earl of Oxford, has become the front runner, although no one seems to have revealed why he should have published his lesser works under his own name and his major ones under the name of an actor from Stratford-upon-Avon. De Vere died in 1604, some eleven years before the last play bearing William Shakespeare's name was written. Did he thoughtfully provide a cache of some fourteen plays for the actor to continue to pass off as his own?

De Vere was not always the frontrunner. That role was initially fulfilled by Sir Francis Bacon, thanks to the strenuous and obsessive efforts of an American namesake of independent means. Delia Bacon appears to have been the first to have suggested that anyone other than the Bard wrote the works – the best part of two and a half centuries after the supposed poet's death. In fact Bacon was surprisingly unconversant with his own putative works. At the trial of conspirators in the Essex rebellion of 1601, he confused the play of *Richard II* with that of *Richard III*.

According to the American writer Nathaniel Hawthorne, Delia Bacon was irresistibly drawn to Stratford 'by the magnetism of those rich secrets, which she supposed to have been hidden by Bacon, or Raleigh, or I know not who, in Shakespeare's grave'. In 1856 she took humble lodgings there 'and began to haunt the church like a ghost'. She must have bribed the notably corrupt sexton for the key of the church for one night she gained entry and groped her way up the aisle to Shakespeare's grave. 'If the divine poet really wrote the inscription and cared as much for the quiet of his bones as his deprecatory earnestness would imply', wrote Hawthorne, 'it was time for those crumbling relics to bestir themselves under her sacrilegious feet.' She made no attempt to disturb the grave, although she satisfied herself that she could lift the tombstone.

> Had she been subject to superstitious terrors, it is impossible to conceive of a situation that could better entitle her to feel them, for, if Shakespeare's ghost would rise at under any provocation, it must have shown itself then, but it is my sincere belief, that, if his figure had appeared within the scope of her dark lantern ... she would have met him fearlessly and controverted his claim to the authorship of the plays to his very face.

Miss Bacon became a recluse, remaining in her room for days. It was only with great difficulty that her landlady, Mrs Baldwin, persuaded her to eat. When a contribution she sent to *The Times* was rejected, she attempted suicide and the Baldwins had to sit with her all night. Next morning they called the doctor. The windows were boarded up to prevent her throwing herself out and she was watched day and night. Before her worst attacks, she read and recited from the Bible and engaged in edifying conversation, but afterwards relapsing into violent and abusive language. When the Baldwins could cope no longer, she was removed to a private asylum in Henley-in-Arden. In 1858 a nephew in the US Navy took her back to America, where she died soon after.

Had Delia Bacon lifted her eyes from Shakespeare's tombstone to his monument, she would have been confronted with the unanimous verdict of his contemporaries that he wrote the works. The first line of his Latin epitaph considers him to share the genius of Socrates and the art of the poet Virgil. A further inscription in English reads:

> Stay passenger, why goest thov by so fast,
> Read if thov canst whom enviovs death hath plast
> With in this monvment shakespeare : with whome,
> Qvick natvre dide: whose name, doth deck ys tombe
> Far more, then cost: sieh all, yt he hath writt,
> Leaves living art bvt page, to serve his witt

A comparison to Virgil? All living art a mere servant to his genius? The case can surely rest.

The Doctor Who Realised That Scurvy is a Vitamin Deficiency Disease

Before the altar at Holy Trinity are arrayed the graves of William Shakespeare and various members of his family. They were not buried here because of his enduring fame, but because he was a tithe holder, whose investment brought funding to the church. Yet it is because of that said fame that they remain here rather than being disinterred after a period of years and their bones placed in the charnel house. That building is long demolished but its small door to the left of the altar is a reminder of its existence. People started to visit the church to pay homage to him soon after his death and the flow of visitors continues to this day. Most gaze intently at his grave and read its famous inscription and glance at the other tombs without realising that Shakespeare's son-in-law, John Hall, is worthy of recognition in his own right.

Hall was what would now be called a homeopathic doctor. The church registers record the death of 'John Hall, gent. *medicus peritissimus*' ('most skilled doctor') on 25 November 1635. His huge professional reputation is confirmed by his description on his tombstone as '*medica celeberrimus arte*' ('most celebrated in the art of medicine'). After his death his casebooks were edited and published with the curious title of *Select Observations on English Bodies*. The editor James Cooke wrote that Hall 'had the happiness to lead the way to that practice almost generally used by the most knowing, of mixing scorbutics in most remedies: it was then ... thought so strange that it was cast as a reproach on him by those most famous in the profession'. Long before such terms were categorised, Hall realised that scurvy was a deficiency disease. His cure, a mixture of scurvy grass, watercress, brooklime, juniper berries and wormwood, rich in vitamins, cured many sufferers. The casebooks reveal that the eldest son of Mr Underhill of Loxley, aged twelve, bore the excruciating agonies that torments those inflicted with this harrowing disease.

> On the right side he had a tumor without discoloration, so I judged there was a tumor of the liver. He was grown as lean as a skeleton, was melancholy, with black and crusty ulcers appearing on his legs. He had a loathing of meat, a disposition to vomit and an Eratic Fever, his urine was red, as in a burning fever, yet without thirst or desire to drink.

That this collection of abominations was cured demonstrates Hall's intuitive brilliance.

On 5 June 1607 John Hall married Susanna, the elder daughter of William and Anne Shakespeare. Her tomb is next to her husband's. Her charming epitaph speaks of her empathy with those in distress and her charitable nature:

> Witty above her sexe, but that's not all,
> Wise to salvation was good Mistres Hall.
> Something of Shakespeare was in that, but this
> Wholey of him with whom she's now in blisse
> Then, passenger, has't ne'er a teare
> To weepe with her that wept with all
> That wept, yet set herself to chere
> Them up with comforts cordiall
> Her love shall live, her mercy spread
> When thou has't ne'er a tear to shed.

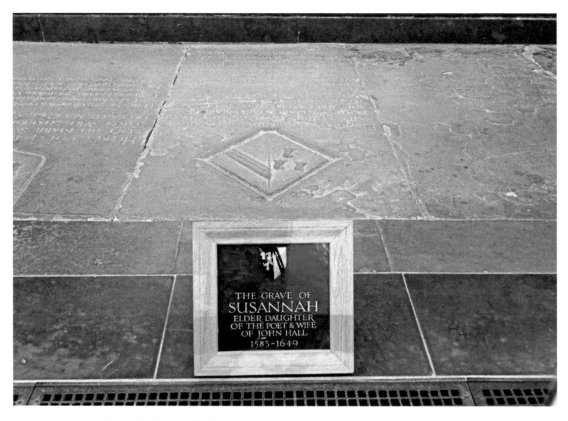

Susanna Hall's tomb (here spelled Susannah).

The word 'witty' in this context does not denote humour, but intelligence. We still use the word in this way when we speak of living off one's wits, or, as Susanna's father put it, 'Brevity is the soul of wit.' It was probably Shakespeare's clever daughter who wrote the Latin epitaph on her mother's tombstone: '*Ubera, tu mater, tu lac vitamque dedisti*' ('With your breasts, mother, you gave me milk and life'). Who else could have written this, apart from her sister, Judith?

Susanna died on 11 July 1649, fifteen years after her husband. Whoever wrote her epitaph added a further two lines in Latin to his, 'What was missing from his tomb was his loyal spouse. She too is his companion now in death.'

The Font in Which William Shakespeare was Baptised
On 26 April 1564 the parish clerk wrote an entry in Latin in the baptismal register at Holy Trinity: '*Guiliamus filius Johannes Shakspere*' ('William, son of John Shakspere'). Both tradition and common sense say that the baby was born three days earlier. The high rate of infant mortality made it customary to baptise babies as rapidly as possible after birth. As cradle Catholics, John and Mary Shakespeare may have believed in the concept of Limbo: the idea that the souls of unbaptised babies go to their own corner of Purgatory. In fact this was never Catholic teaching, but it was widely believed.

The medieval font was probably removed from the church in 1747, when a new one was installed. It came into the possession of the parish clerk, who used it as a water butt in his garden in Church Street. In 1823 it came into the possession of the mayor, James Saunders, a captain in the local militia. As the keen and skilled local antiquarian he would have realised its significance. In 1861 it was purchased by the town clerk, William Hunt, who restored it to the church. It now stands in its battered condition in the chancel, close to facsimiles of the entries in the register for Shakespeare's birth and death. Its service for non-baptismal duties has taken its toll, but it remains an evocative object for visitors to the church.

The Shakespeares must have feared for the survival of their firstborn son, for they had already baptised and lost two daughters. These fears were compounded when on 11 July the vicar, John Bretchgirdle, entered the name in the burial register of Oliver Gunn, an apprentice weaver, with the ominous words, '*Hic incipit pestis*' ('Here begins the plague').

Shakespeare's baptismal entry.

By the end of that year, around one eighth of the population had been carried off. Fortunately for posterity, one of these was not William Shakespeare.

The Stone Altar

In 1889 workmen engaged in installing the new organ at Holy Trinity made the remarkable discovery of a stone altar, or *mensa*, beneath the floor. It had originally graced the Chapel of St Thomas of Canterbury in the chantry (where prayers were said for the souls of the dead) in the south aisle. The altar still carries three of its five original crosses. These represent the five places where it was anointed during its consecration, symbolising the five Holy Wounds of Christ.

How the altar came to be so concealed is a mystery. It is most likely that the very concealment symbolises one of the fiercest arguments of the Reformation – that of the nature of the Eucharist. To Catholics the stone altar was a place of sacrifice where the Passion of Christ was recreated in his living presence. Protestants rejected this, believing that Holy Communion was a memorial meal, following Christ's instruction to 'do this in memory of me'. Hence stone altars were an anathema and were ordered to be removed, but when did this happen to the stone altar at Holy Trinity? It could have happened in

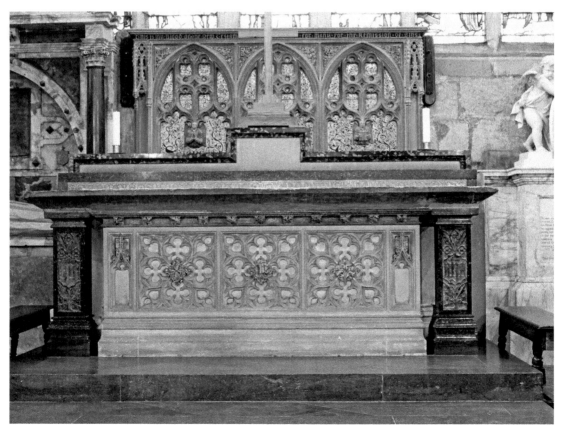

Stone altar.

response to the Ecclesiastical Commissioners in the reign of Edward VI, but if that were so, its concealment would have been well remembered during the reign of the Catholic Mary I and it would have been restored to its place. Most likely it happened at the beginning of the reign of Elizabeth and after the passing of the Act of Uniformity of 1559, when it was decreed that 'all signs of superstition and idolatry' be removed from churches and even from private houses. In the Book of Common Prayer there is no mention of the word 'altar' – the words 'Holy Table' are used instead. If the altar was removed then, it was probably in the hope of an eventual Catholic succession of which there was some hope.

At the time that the altar was rediscovered, the Church of England was undergoing another period of dramatic change with the Oxford Movement seeking to recover some of the ancient 'Catholic Truths' to the Church. The formidable vicar George Arbuthnot had sympathies with this cause. Under his guidance, the stone was placed on the High Altar. It is one of the few surviving medieval stone altars to be found in Britain.

14. The Public School That Never Was

For over thirty years Trinity College was the best-known school in Stratford – founded in 1872 by the vicar. Dr Collis achieved a national reputation as a campaigner against the then prevalent elaborate funerals that contributed to the further impoverishment of the poor, founding the National Burial Reform Committee.

Dr Collis also roused controversy in his doctrinal views. A firm Anglo-Catholic, in the days when 'the Protestant Religion' was a regular after-dinner toast, he lamented what he saw as the destruction wrought by the Reformation. 'But for the ill-fated sacrilege of Henry VIII', he wrote, 'there would have been ample revenues for the work of the church in Stratford. His Catholic neo-medievalism inspired a grand plan to reproduce Holy Trinity Church's collegiate establishment of the fourteenth century. He founded a parochial organisation for the care of the sick and poor, and raised the money to establish a nursing home for women and children. Part of his grand scheme was Trinity College, which opened with a staff of able teachers and twenty-two pupils, in a large house he acquired and extended in Church Street. Soon it was attended by boarders from all over the country and boasted admissions to the universities and scholarships to leading public schools. Emphasis was based on the boys' backgrounds as this helped recruitment, but he was not an elitist. He intended that one tenth of the places should be given without fees, a pattern established by his own headmaster and mentor, Dr Thomas Arnold, at Rugby.

The school became very much part of Stratford's life. After the death of Dr Collis it became the Army School, with the objective of preparing boys for service life. Among its alumni were the actor/playwright Stephen Phillips and the cartoonist Bruce Bairnsfather. It appeared destined to become part of the national educational establishment, but this reckoned without the arrival next door of Marie Corelli. The novelist and the boys were soon at odds. She complained about the noise and the footballs that came hurtling over the fence into her garden. Despite the efforts of Mr Beckwith, the headmaster, the more Marie complained, the more provocative the boys became. According to the childhood memories of the novelist Ursula Bloom, a boy named Skinner nearly blew himself up while attempting to bombard Miss Corelli's new winter garden with a starting cannon bought from Mr Smith's shop in the High Street. Nemesis was due. In 1908 Marie struck, purchasing the paddock behind the school that it leased as a playing field. Life under such a landlady would be intolerable. A site was purchased in Maidenhead. As the boys moved out, they broke Marie's windows. Stratford's shopkeepers were furious. The school was a good source of trade. Today the Grade II-listed building is occupied by flats. The only reminder of this noted academy is the inscription placed by Dr Collis in the eaves:

Collegium sanctae et
Individuae trinitatis
Ad mdccclccii.

15. The House of the Bestselling of All Victorian Novelists

In 1899 the popular novelist Marie Corelli moved to Stratford, renting Hall's Croft, the former home of Shakespeare's son-in-law. She was at the peak of her popularity after the publication of such books as *Barabbas* and *The Sorrows of Satan*. The sales were enhanced by her gifts for controversy, self-publicity and the myths she made up about herself. She claimed to be a descendent of the Italian musician and composer Arcangelo Corelli, and would lapse into odd snatches of Italian (E. F. Benson's character, Lucia, is partially based on her). In fact she was born Minnie Mackay, the illegitimate daughter of the noted journalist and songwriter Charles Mackay and his housekeeper. She was among the first to adopt the practice of doctoring photographs to send to her many fans, making her look younger and more glamorous than she really was. Her stay in Stratford got off to an unfortunate start. Opposite Hall's Croft was a private girls' school run by the formidable Mrs Cameron Stuart. All day Old Town resonated with the lasses' chatter and the tinkling of pianos. Miss Corelli sent over a curt note requesting silence – she was working on *Boy*, her latest masterpiece. The reply was correct but negative and a furious Marie moved to 'Avoncroft' further down the street.

In light of the above incident, it is astonishing that Marie should choose to move to Mason Croft in Church Street, which was situated next to Trinity College; but move she did, together with her lifelong companion, Bertha Vyver, in 1900. She imposed her own personality on the building. The dining room was converted into a music room (Marie had had genuine aspirations to be a concert pianist). The massive fireplace still bears the intertwined initials 'M.C.' and 'B.V.', surrounded by laurel leaves and bearing the inscription *'Amor Vincit'* ('Love Conquers').

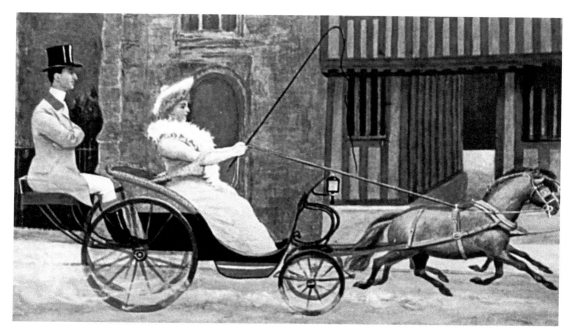

Marie Corelli.

Marie's flamboyance made her a local celebrity. Her fame attracted crowds to stand on the pavement opposite her house. On Shakespeare's birthday she laid an enormous wreath of flowers, gathered in Dante's garden in Florence, on his grave. Celebrities flocked to her door, including Winston Churchill, Sarah Bernhardt, the singer Clara Butt, Ellen Terry and Mark Twain. She and Bertha would ride round Stratford in a miniature chaise pulled by two Shetland ponies named Puck and Ariel. She would boat on the Avon in a gondola imported from Venice, complete with gondaleer. Cabdrivers pointed out Mason Croft as Stratford's prime attraction. Even the American visitors, as *Punch* wittily observed, were diverted:

> The Yankee streaming to the Shrine
> Of the Immortal Mummer,
> Forgets the dead and doubtful 'Swan'
> And concentrates his worship on
> The real and living Hummer.

Marie was well before her time, being what would now be termed 'a conservationist'. She desired to 'lovingly and sacredly guard every old building and the form of all Stratford's old streets'. She saved old cottages on Waterside and lovingly restored the Tudor House, a half-timbered building on the corner of Ely Street and the High Street. She persuaded Harvard University to acquire the beautiful building that had once been the home of Katherine Rogers, the mother of John Harvard, the university's founder. Her efforts to conserve Stratford's heritage were not always appreciated locally, as was demonstrated when the American industrialist and philanthropist Andrew Carnegie proposed to demolish three ancient dilapidated cottages close to Shakespeare's birthplace in Henley Street. Marie vehemently opposed this, although it was clear that many in Stratford were keen to get the library. Marie's fury knew no bounds when the *Stratford-upon-Avon Herald* published a letter casting doubts on her motives and she sued George Boyden, the proprietor of the paper, and the writer of the letter, Fred Winter, a local draper, for libel. The action against Boyden was later dropped, but the case against Winter was heard in a Birmingham court with the gallery packed with Stratfordians keen to partake of this free entertainment. Marie won her case, but the damages were merely 'the smallest coin of the realm, one farthing'. As it happened, Marie gained the last laugh. An obscure by-law forbade the destruction of any properties that had belonged to Shakespeare's family and it was discovered that the cottages had once belonged to his son-in-law, Thomas Quiney. Threats of further legal action produced a sensible compromise and the library was established in the heavily restored cottages.

Marie's war with Trinity College was her last foray into controversy. As her literary star waned, she ceased to be involved in the town's squabbles. Yet her personality had inspired a kind of affection in Stratford, and at her funeral in 1924 the pavements were crowded with local people paying their last respects to a woman who had made life in the town more colourful. Bertha lived on at Mason Croft until her death in 1939, after which Marie intended that a trust should be formed to preserve the house 'for the promotion of Science, Literature and Music among the people of Stratford-upon-Avon'. It was probably the memory of an imagined slight from Sir Frank Benson that led to her insistence that 'all persons connected with the stage be excluded from the premises'. In fact, dwindling royalties ensured that the trust was never formed. In 1951 Mason Croft was acquired by the University of Birmingham to house its Shakespeare Institute, which is probably as close as it's possible to get to fulfilling Marie's intentions, although whether she would have approved of the library building added in 1996 must be open to doubt. A conservationist to the last, she was keen to pursue what she regarded as Stratford's best interests, even if the locals did not always realise it themselves, she intended that the garden and paddock be preserved as 'a breathing space and air zone for the health of the town ... now endangered by the overcrowding of buildings entirely disadvantageous to the well being of the population'. This at least has been fulfilled, and children from the nearby Broad Street School still play sports and games in Marie's paddock.

16. The Waiter's Tab

Stratford-upon-Avon is a new town. Not one like Welwyn Garden City or Milton Keynes, but a new town nonetheless. The first extant reference to the place comes when Egwin, bishop of the Hwiccas,[1] exchanged a religious house at Fladbury for one held by the King of Mercia at 'Aet-Stratford' ('the Isle of the Ford'). The original Stratford was a small settlement clustered near this monastery, which presumably was located where Holy Trinity Church

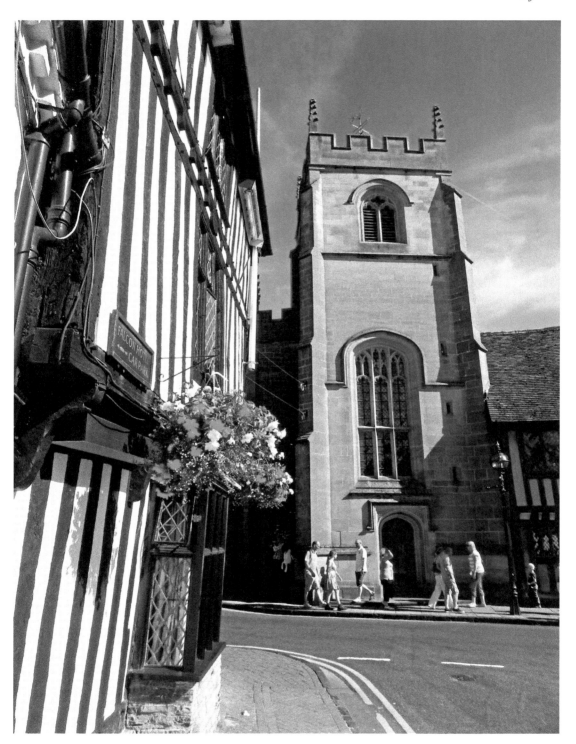

Guild Chapel from the Falcon Hotel.

now stands. At the end of the twelfth century a new town came into being. With its grid of wide, regular streets, Stratford has the air of a planned town. It was perhaps the building of a wooden bridge over the Avon that caused those responsible for diocesan finances to see the potential of the river crossing linking the rich pastures of the Forest of Arden with the uplands of the Cotswold and Feldon. The new settlement was a religious foundation, governed by several guilds of which the most important was the Guild of the Holy Cross. In 1269 Godfrey Gifford, the Bishop of Worcester, granted this guild permission to build a hospice, which still exists as the almshouses and the Guild Chapel. These were eventually linked by a schoolroom, from which developed King Edward's School and a Guild Hall, which represented the start of local government in Stratford. This was where the brothers and sisters held their annual feast. On one such occasion, a waiter jotted a list of orders on the wall, where it can still be seen today, together with fifteenth-century wall paintings, which have been uncovered by a recent restoration of the fabric.

With the abolition of religious orders in 1547, the Guild Hall became the meeting place of the newly formed Borough Council in 1553. It was here that John Shakespeare, the poet's father, would have been installed as the bailiff (mayor) in 1568 and it is here that it is likely his son would have seen his first play, since it was the custom for travelling companies to put on a special performance for the leading citizens and their families. It is significant that it is during John Shakespeare's bailiwick that companies of actors are first recorded as playing in Stratford.

17. The Oldest Schoolroom in the Land

Most of the buildings of the Guild of the Holy Cross were reconstructed between 1468 and 1480. It was in this period that the Guildhall and the schoolroom above it were built. A notable endowment came from a wealthy priest of the guild, Thomas Jolyffe, who in 1482 gave his property in Stratford and Dodwell to provide an annual salary of £10 for a priest 'to teach grammar freely to all the scholars coming to the school, taking nothing of the scholars for their teaching'. There was a school in existence before this. Among those ordained deacons in 1295 was Richard, rector of the school, but Thomas Jolyffe's endowment is the earliest record of the institution that was to become the King Edward VI Grammar School. After the Protestant Reformation the school was reconstituted in 1555, when the successors of the guild, the Stratford Corporation, resolved to appoint 'a lawful and honest man lerned in gramr and in the lawe of god'. William Smart was paid an annual salary of £20 to 'gently dyly to employ himself, with such godly wysdom and lernyinge as God hathe and shale endue hym with, to lerne and teche in the saide gramer scole such scholars and chylder as shall ... come together to lerne godly lernyinge and wisdom, beying fet for the gramer scole.'

It was in the schoolroom upstairs that William Shakespeare must have been taught. Whatever debts he owed to his formative years, he appears to have viewed his schooldays with the lack of enthusiasm of his 'whining schoolboy, with his satchel/ And shining morning face, creeping like snail/ unwillingly to school'.

The room contains a teacher's chair and old oak desks. One of them even has the initials 'WS' carved into it, but unfortunately this was not the work of the Bard – the desks date from the eighteenth century.

The Guildhall and schoolroom recently received a Heritage Lottery grant of £1.4 million towards their restoration. Over 600 years since they were first created, they continue to provide a place of education for Stratford boys.

18. Doomsday

In his last will and testament of 1498, Stratford's great benefactor, Sir Hugh Clopton, left instructions for the rebuilding of the Guild Chapel. He required the roof to be covered with glazing 'and all other fornyshments thereunto necessary to it, to be paide by my saide executors as the workis aforesaid goeth fourth'. This included wall paintings. On the ceiling were scenes from the history of the Holy Cross; on the walls, pictures of the martyrdom of St Thomas Becket and St George and the dragon. Above the chancel was a great painting of the Last Judgement – doomsday. Its graphic gaping devils dragging the lost souls to hellfire and perdition contrasted with the blessed ascending to glory. It must have brought fascinated terror to children and served as an unneeded *momento mori* to the sick and infirm who chiefly used this chapel of ease. William Shakespeare may have recalled this painting in Puck's speech in *A Midsummer Night's Dream*:

> Now it is the time of night
> That the graves, all gaping wide,
> Every one lets forth a sprite
> In the church-way paths to glide.

But that is to assume that they were still there for him to see. In the year before his birth, his father, John Shakespeare, as borough chamberlain, paid for the pictures to be painted over, presumably as part of the actions of removing vestiges of Catholicism from religious buildings. Yet it is unclear which paintings received this treatment. In 1634 Stratford Corporation, in the midst of an acrimonious dispute with Thomas Wilson, the vicar, complained that he had 'profaned the Guild Chapel by suffering the pictures therein to be defaced'. Since Wilson was a fervent Puritan, this is hardly surprising, but it does imply that at least some of the paintings had survived.

Whoever it was who painted over the murals employed limewash, which was removable. They were rediscovered in 1804 when the chapel was being refurbished. A local historian, R. W. Wheler, noted that they were 'found to be in a nearly perfect state'. They were covered up again, but not before a watercolourist had recorded their

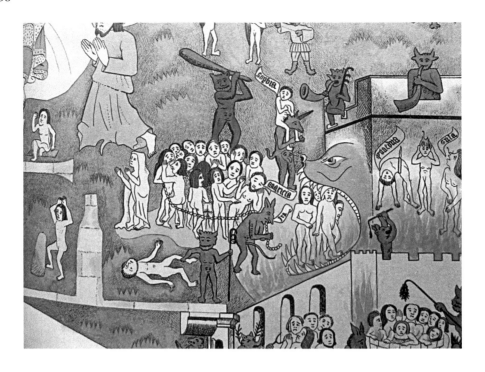

Above and below: Paintings in Guild Chapel.

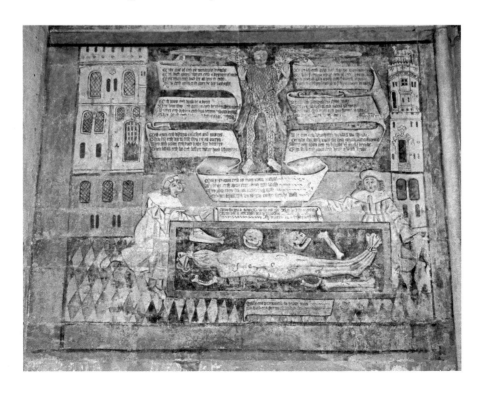

detail and colouring. When they were uncovered again in 1928 by E. W. Tristam, an authority on medieval wall paintings, they had deteriorated significantly. In the 1950s the paintings that were in poor repair were protected by wooden panels, which are only opened occasionally. In 2016 a project named 'Death Reawakened' commenced work on the restoration of these paintings to their former splendour, helped by a grant of £100,000 from the Heritage Lottery Fund.

19. The Roof of Shakespeare's House

In 1597 William Shakespeare bought New Place, 'a pratty house of brick and timber'. It had been built by Sir Hugh Clopton in 1483 and was probably the first brick-built house in Stratford. When Shakespeare bought it, however, it was in a state of 'great ruine and decay and unrepayred'. Extensive work was necessary, and in 1598 'Mr Shaxpere' sold the Corporation 'a lod of ston', which was probably surplus to his requirements. It became a strong local tradition that the mulberry tree growing in the courtyard had been planted by the poet's own hand. It was from New Place that the poet's cortege must have departed, two days after his death on 23 April 1616. The house passed to his daughter, Susanna, and her husband, the physician John Hall.

At the beginning of the Civil War in July 1642, Stratford's bells rang out as Queen Henrietta Maria arrived at the head of an army of 2,000 foot and 1,000 horse, with artillery. She was met by Prince Rupert with another force and lodged at New Place with the widowed Susanna Hall. The expenses of the visit fell upon the beleaguered Corporation, which paid out £18 6s for 'when the Queen Majastye lay in the town'.

With the death of Shakespeare's granddaughter and last descendent, Lady Elizabeth Barnard, in 1670, the house eventually passed back to the original owners. Sir Hugh Clopton, like his namesake and forebear, possessed great generosity of spirit, delighting in showing New Place and its famous mulberry tree to visitors. Three such arrived there in the summer of 1744: the celebrated David Garrick, only twenty-three but already in the first flush of his fame, accompanied by his fellow actors Denis Delane and Charles Macklin. Neither Garrick nor Stratford could know how their futures were intertwined.

Sir Hugh was an heir to the aristocratic tradition of freely opening their mansions to the curious. Revd Francis Gastrell, a canon of Lichfield Cathedral, acquired New Place in 1753 but felt 'no sort of pride or pleasure in this charming retirement, no consciousness of being possessed of the sacred ground which the Muses had consecrated to the memory of their favourite poet'. He was soon at war with Stratford, even stirring the Corporation from its lethargy by indulging in long wrangles over the Poor Rate, to which demands he had contributed by evicting tenants. Matters were exacerbated by the steady tramp of visitors who sought to see the celebrated mulberry tree, which he considered to cut out the light from his windows and make the house damp. One night in 1756 he screwed his courage to

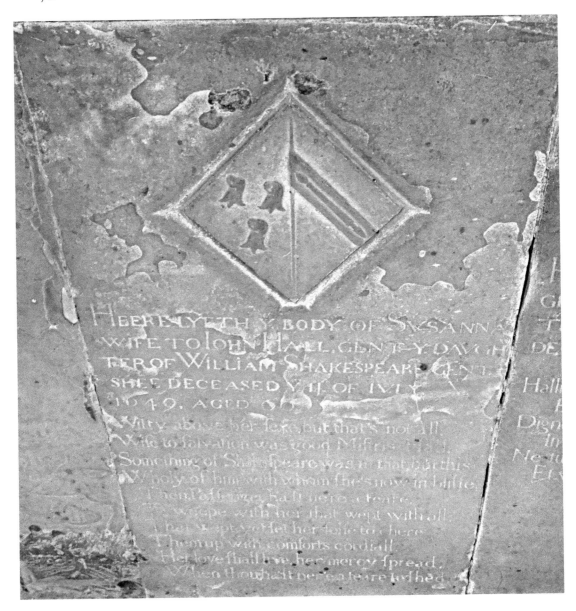

Susanna's tomb.

the chopping place. The next morning all that remained of the sacred tree was a pile of logs in the yard. The reaction of the Stratfordians to this sacrilege was to break 'the reverend destroyer's windows'. Amid the fury, one man realised his hour had come. Thomas Sharpe, clock winder to the Corporation, bought the remains of the tree. He was to create sufficient souvenirs from the 'original' wood to consume entire groves of mulberry trees.

All was not over between Parson Gastrell and the Corporation. When a further effort was made to extract the full Poor Rate, despite his frequent absences, he vowed: *'that* house should never be assessed again.' In 1759 he razed New Place to the ground and left Stratford forever, 'amidst the rage and curses of the inhabitants'. According to one report, the populace vowed never to allow anyone of the same name to enter the precincts of the town ever again. It was fortunate that the perpetrator of this outrage was not a Smith or a Jones.

Perhaps out of respect to the memory of the Bard, no new building was ever erected on the vacant site of New Place. All that remains of the building today are the well shaft, the arches that formed one wall of the cellar and, yes, the outline of its roof on the side wall of Nash's House next door.

20. The Sculptures That Once Graced Pall Mall

Behind the site of the demolished house lies the exquisite Great Garden of New Place, noted for its beautiful Elizabethan knot garden, its tunnel arbour of trained fruit trees, the inevitable mulberry tree, said to be a scion of the one that the wicked Parson Gaskell chopped down, beautifully maintained flower beds, lovely mature trees and trimmed lawns.

The eye of the visitor may be caught by the huge monument to Shakespeare that stands at the south end of the gardens. The sculpted relief shows the poet, flanked by the muses of Drama and Poetry. Few, if any, will realise that this creation has an interesting story to tell: that of John Boydell, an engraver and publisher who conceived, amid the rising tide of patriotism in the eighteenth century, a desire to create a School of British Historical Painting. This coincided with a surge in the popularity of Shakespeare's plays that had been created by editors like Samuel Johnson and actors like David Garrick. The first part of the project was to create a grand edition of Shakespeare, illustrated by the finest artists of the day. The idea was conceived at a dinner where such contemporary luminaries as the renowned painters Benjamin West and George Romney attended.

The large volume would contain seventy-two prints that could be bought separately in a folder. It was decided to open a gallery to exhibit the paintings from which the prints were taken. A subscription was opened to raise the huge sum required to finance the ambitious project. The participants would make a down payment and pay the remainder on delivery. In June 1788, Boydell and his nephew bought the prestigious address of No. 52 Pall Mall as the site for the gallery. George Dance, a founding member of the Royal Academy, was commissioned as the architect. Work began on the handsome volumes of the *Complete Works*. The leading Shakespeare scholar, George Steevens, was appointed as the general editor. It was a huge enterprise; a printing works was established and a foundry to cast the new typeface that had been specially designed for the project. A small factory was established to manufacture the ink. The first volume was published in 1791. The rest

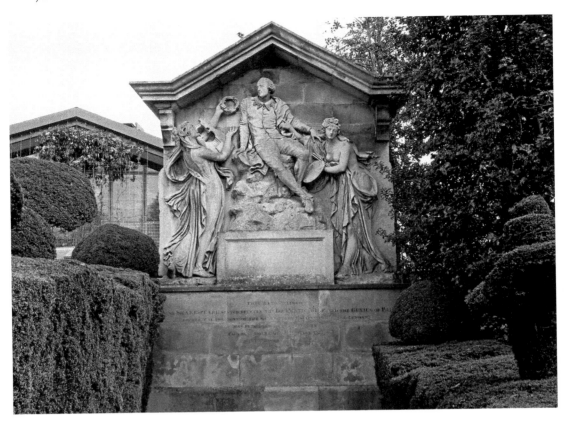

Alto Relivo, New Palace Gardens.

followed over the next fourteen years. Boydell commissioned some of the most eminent artists of the day to create works for the gallery, including Romney, Henry Fuseli, West, John Opie, Francesco Bartolozzi and one of the two female founders of the Royal Academy, the Swiss artist Angelika Kaufmann.

George Dance produced a handsome design for Boydell's Shakespeare Gallery, with a full-length exhibition hall on the ground floor and three smaller ones upstairs. The neoclassical stone frontage featured a large central recess into which was placed a huge sculpture – yes, of Shakespeare and the muses. In close proximity to the sculpture is a column from the Town Hall of the 1640s.

21. The Room Where It All Began

In 1824 fifteen Stratfordians 'humble in rank, but enthusiastic in their admiration of the Immortal Poet' sat down to a luncheon at the Falcon Hotel on Shakespeare's birthday. Thus was founded the Stratford-upon-Avon Shakespeare Club – the oldest such in the world. Appropriately, the original members were not from learned bodies or the theatre, but drawn from the same class of local artisans as the poet. They included James George, a grocer, William Sheldon, a plumber and glazier, Samuel King, an upholsterer, and Charles Green, a hatter. Although the club split into two factions, the annual Shakespeare's birthday lunch was soon attended by over 200 people. The club had a great success in 1827 when it organised a considerable festival, which included many of the elements of David Garrick's famous event of 1759 – a costumed procession, fireworks and a masquerade ball. Later that year, an even more significant occasion occurred: the opening of the Royal Shakespearean Theatre in the Great Garden of New Place. This – Stratford's first system-built theatre – was the brainchild of the well-known comic actor Charles Mathews, but the support of the Shakespeare clubs was vital to the project. Some of the greatest names in English stage history played there, including W. C. Macready, Edmund Kean and Charles Booth. The idea of theatre in Stratford was established. The clubs organised an even bigger festival in 1830 and so the idea of a celebration on Shakespeare's birthday was firmly planted.

The room in which this luncheon, which led to so much, must have been held is through the front door of the Falcon and into the first door on the left. It is now known as the Scholars' Room.

22. The Day They Tried to Blow Up the Town Hall

On the small back wall of Stratford Town Hall, adjacent to the Shakespeare Hotel, a plaque presented by the re-enactment group, Colonel George Monck's Regiment of Foote, commemorates the 350th anniversary of the English Civil War. It recalls a time when Stratford was at the centre of military action. On 23 October 1642 the town had echoed to the noise of gunfire during the Battle of Edgehill. After the battle there was the sound of tramping feet and the clatter of horses' hooves as the retreating Parliamentary army fell back on Warwick.

Stratford's place on the frontline was not over. Indeed, it had hardly begun. Early in 1643 a troop of Royalist horse commanded by Colonel Wagstaffe occupied the town and recruited a number of locals to the king's cause. On 25 February the principal local antagonist on the Parliamentary side, Lord Brooke, advanced from his stronghold at Warwick Castle and resolved on a surprise attack. 'Yet a countryman and friend of theirs', recorded the Parliamentary chronicler, 'espying us two miles on this side, crossed the fields and gave the enemy advertisement: upon which they drew themselves out under a hill, where they could view us in our march ... we drew up our reere, so that we stood triangle upon three hils in full view of each other. From the reer division we let flie a drake, which ran through the midst of them and forced them to wheele off towards the Town.' Faced by superior firepower, Wagstaffe retreated, leaving two dead behind. His local recruits had fled at the first sign of danger.

The Parliamentarians had not heard the last of Wagstaffe. Learning that a military council was to be held in the Town Hall, which sheltered an ammunition dump, he crept into town and laid a 'traine of powder to a piece of match left at such a length as should … just meet the powder at the time of their sitting'. The building went up, but prematurely:

When they thought all had been quiet and well and the Lord Brooke and the Colonels and Captains were going to the Council, they heard a noise as if some houses had fallen down and saw the Town Hall in pieces in such a manner that it is utterly ruined, one of the townsmen slaine and four more burnt and bruised, who are very ill … O the great cause we have to praise God for such deliverances as these!

23. The Mysterious Date on the Town Hall

On the façade of Stratford's Town Hall the words 'God Save The King' are emblazoned in large letters. When our present queen succeeded to the throne, the Borough Council was

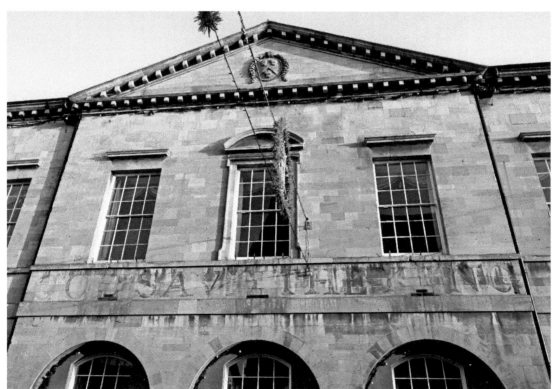

'God Save the King' on the Town Hall.

inundated with suggestions that this wording should be changed, so they added the date when the inscription was painted: 1769 – the year that the great actor David Garrick held a jubilee in honour of William Shakespeare in the town.

The jubilee and the Town Hall were intimately linked. By the 1760s the old building was in danger of collapse, yet the Corporation lacked the resources to rebuild it. Francis Wheler, Stratford's recorder, hit upon the means to resolve the issue. Hearing of Garrick's adoration of anything Shakespearean and his susceptibility to grand flattery, he thought that it would be 'an ornament' to the Town Hall if he could be persuaded to donate a 'Handsom present'. A means towards this might be to make him an honorary burgess. The upshot was that the actor resolved not only to present Stratford with the desired statue, but to hold a jubilee in honour of Shakespeare there. The centrepiece would be a great rotunda, specially erected for the occasion, on the banks of the Avon. Jubilee fever gripped London. On 1 September David and Eva-Maria Garrick set out, followed by a great convoy of actors and musicians. 'All the inns and roads from London are filled', declared a traveller, 'as if an army was on the march.'

Garrick had commissioned the sculptor John Cheere to produce a life-sized statue of Shakespeare. This would have the place of honour in the rotunda, where the actor

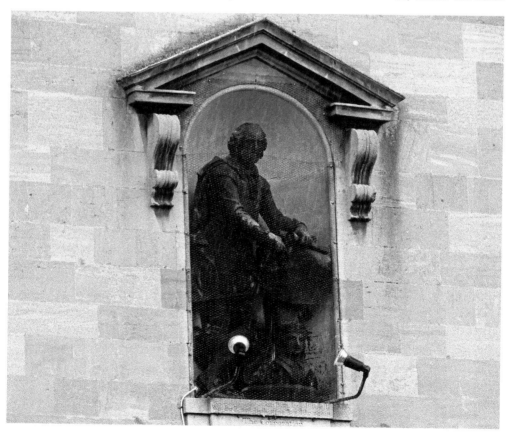

Shakespeare, the Town Hall.

would recite the ode that he had composed to Shakespeare. In return, the Corporation had agreed to commission a portrait of the great actor. His choice fell on Thomas Gainsborough, despite his misgivings that the artist did not demonstrate sufficient reverence towards the Bard. As well as picking up the bill for the portrait, the burghers had to pay out for the frame created by Thomas Davies of Edgbaston, who also carved the inevitable box of mulberry wood in which the freedom of the town was to be presented. The number of events for the jubilee was impressive. There would be a masked ball, a civic banquet, a Shakespearean procession, a firework display and a horserace. In the spirit of the occasion, a real effort was made by the townspeople to decorate their houses appropriately for the occasion and this was enhanced by the efforts of Garrick's scenic wizard, his brother George, who created great transparencies to adorn prominent buildings. It was probably he and his team who created the patriotic lettering that can still be seen on the Town Hall.

In the event, the one part of the organisation that could neither be controlled nor predicted brought nemesis to the occasion. The weather turned against Garrick: the heavens opened and the River Avon burst its banks. The ode was a great success and Garrick made up for his losses by putting on a show about the jubilee on the London stage that mercilessly lampooned his fellow burgesses – the Stratfordians. Although it was not realised at the time, the Corporation got infinite value for its expenditure. Gainsborough created a happy portrait of an elegant Garrick embracing an amiable bust of Shakespeare. Sadly this was destroyed by a fire in the Town Hall in 1946. John Cheere's sculpture still adorns its niche and George Garrick's lettering remains to puzzle the visitor. For those who wish to gain an idea of what Stratford looked like on jubilee morning, the price of a drink in the Shakespeare Hotel next door will enable the inspection of a large picture illustrating that very occasion.

24. Everyman

Opposite the Town Hall, on a small raised platform, stands a bronze statue of a man bearing the town's coat of arms. He wears a tunic, sandals, breaches and a cloak. His clothing is tattered but he has a dignified bearing. The expression on his face is sad. There is no indication as to who the statue is supposed to be – a comment made by many people ever since its inception in 1964. In fact it is appropriately called *Everyman*, the work of the sculptor Fred J. Kormis, who was born of Jewish parents in Frankfurt-am-Main in 1887. He served as an apprentice to a sculptor and joined the Austro-Hungarian army at the outbreak of the First World War. He was captured in 1915 and spent the next five years in a POW camp in Siberia. After his release he returned to Frankfurt but fled to Holland after the Nazis came to power in 1933. He then went to England, where he anglicised his name from Fritz to Fred. He established his own studio in London but his misfortunes continued to pursue him. The studio was destroyed by bombing in 1940. After the war he achieved a number of noteworthy commissions; and his practice flourished. The statue in Stratford was part of the redevelopment of the Corn Exchange site.

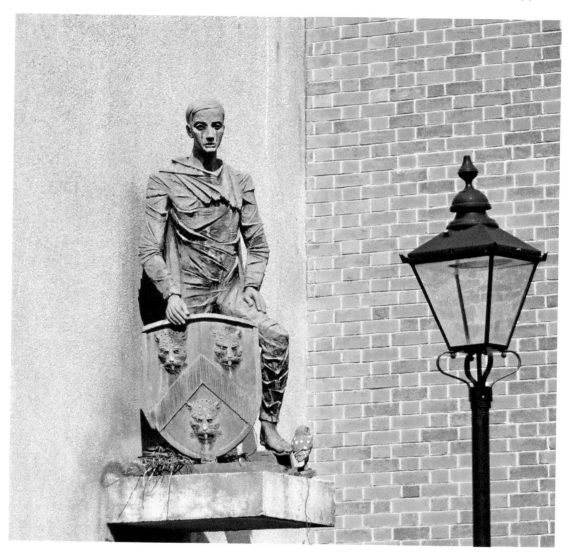

Everyman.

25. The Signed House That Begat America's Oldest University

Elizabethan Stratford was a tinder box of wattle and daub and thatch, a situation compounded by open hearths and the many ovens serving the town's prime economic activity of malting. A great fire that swept away many buildings in 1595 carried with it the house of Thomas Rogers, a wealthy butcher, maltster, grazier and fellow alderman of John Shakespeare on the Borough Council. No expense was spared in rebuilding the house at what is now No. 26 High Street. The more fireproof material of brick was employed and a woodcarver engaged to create a magnificent frontage, along which are carved heads and symbols, the date of the building's erection (1596) and the initials of Thomas Rogers and his second wife, Alice.

Rogers had five baptised children from his first marriage and five from his second. His second child by this marriage, Katherine, was married on 8 April 1605 at Holy Trinity Church at the age of twenty-three to Robert Harvard, a forty-three-year-old butcher from the London district of Southwark. She was his second wife. It is unknown what brought them together, but the most likely point of contact is the trade shared by her father and her husband. She, too, had numerous children, but all but two of them – her sons, John and Thomas – were carried off in the plague year of 1625, together with her husband. Within five months, she had married again – to John Elletson, a wealthy cooper. He died just five months later, leaving his wife the bulk of his property. She married another wealthy man, Richard Yearwood, a cooper and Member of Parliament. He died in 1632, so Katherine inherited another fortune. Her elder son, John, attended Emmanuel College, Cambridge, an

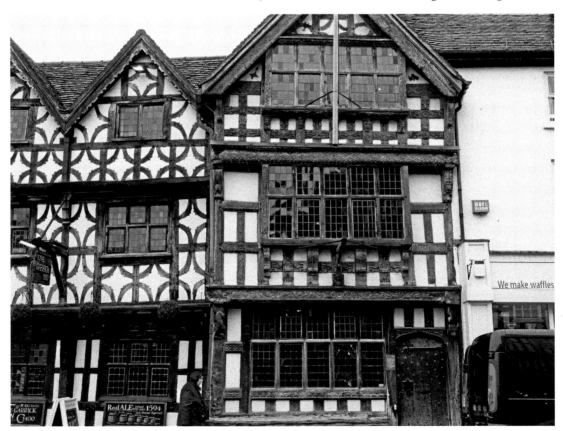

The Garrick pub and Harvard House.

institution noted for its Puritan zeal. He is described in his mother's will as a 'clerk', which implies that he had taken holy orders. He was inspired by the establishment of a Puritan commonwealth in Massachusetts in 1620, for shortly after his marriage he resolved to go there himself, selling property to pay for the voyage. As a scholar, he would have been aware that books were a rare commodity in the new colony, so he took his considerable library with him when they sailed early in 1637. Sadly, his time in the New World was short, for he died in 1638 at the age of thirty-one. He was probably part of a project that was under discussion to establish a centre of higher learning in the colony and left his estate of £779 12s 2d and his library to the furtherance of this cause. It was perhaps in honour of his university that the name of the place where the college was to be established was changed to Cambridge. It is certainly that the foundation that became one of the world's great universities was named in honour of its first benefactor. In 1639, it was ordered 'that the colledge agreed upon shalbe called Harvard Colledge'.

The house of John Harvard's grandparents passed through many ownerships and was the centre of a number of trades before it became the focus of Marie Corelli's desire to preserve Stratford's Tudor heritage. She persuaded Edward Morris, the president of a Chicago meat-packing company, to acquire what had become known as 'The Ancient House' and he later presented it to Harvard University in memory of its founder. In 1990 the Shakespeare Birthplace Trust took over responsibility for this Grade I-listed building. Since 1996 it has housed the Museum of British Pewter.

26. The Wall Paintings Shakespeare Must Have Gazed Upon

In 1927 men working at the White Swan Hotel in Stratford's Rother Market made a remarkable discovery. Beneath layers of paint and wallpaper in the lounge, they found wall paintings from an earlier era. They informed the manager, who, to his credit, halted work immediately and called in expert advice. The three paintings were identified as dating from around 1560 and tell the story from the biblical apocrypha of Tobias and the angel. A bible in a nearby glass case is open at the relevant page. It is a suitably venerable edition, but for some reason is in French.

The largest painting reaches to the ceiling and is subdivided. On either side it is flanked by representations of exotic plants. The central sections show Tobias' mother and Tobit, his blind father, sending him off on an errand to a distant city to collect debts owed to his father. Behind Tobias stands a fourth figure – probably the disguised archangel Raphael, who was to be his companion on his journey. The panel alongside shows Tobias and the disguised Raphael approaching a turreted city – apparently they've also acquired a dog en route. Above the pictures, the text gives a brief commentary on what is happening. Other panels show Tobias catching a huge fish in the River Tigris. The disguised Raphael advises him to retain its heart, liver and gall. These are used to lift a curse on Sarah, who had been engaged to marry seven different men, all of whom had died on the night before the marriage. The curse lifted, Tobias marries Sarah and thanks to the fish, Tobit's blindness is cured. The identity of Raphael is revealed.

Despite some inevitable damage, the paintings are in remarkably fine condition. A letter to *The Times* on 28 July 1927 quoted a report by Philip Johnson, an authority on English murals: 'It may be said that the art quality is exceptionally good, and obviously that of an English artist.' The paintings give a fascinating picture of life and costume in Elizabethan times.

At the time the paintings were created, the inn was called the King's Hall Tavern. It was kept by the probable commissioner of the paintings, Robert Perrott. He had been bailiff of the town in 1558, but subsequently refused to serve on the Corporation. The maintenance of the oligarchical system of local government was dependent on the cooperation of all men of means. The quarrel was discussed over wine and food at The Bear by three local worthies – Sir Thomas Lucy, Clement Throckmorton and Sir Henry Goodere – who had been asked to arbitrate the matter. The burgesses must have felt amply recompensed for their expenditure of 37s 8d when the three gentlemen suggested that Perrott, of his 'free goodwill', pay the £53 6s 8d he owed in back fines and that all thenceforth should 'henceforth be Lovers and ffrends'. Unfortunately, Perrott's goodwill did not extend to paying this enormous sum. In 1567 the Corporation tried to force his hand by electing him as bailiff once more, but he declared that he would never serve again. In his stead,

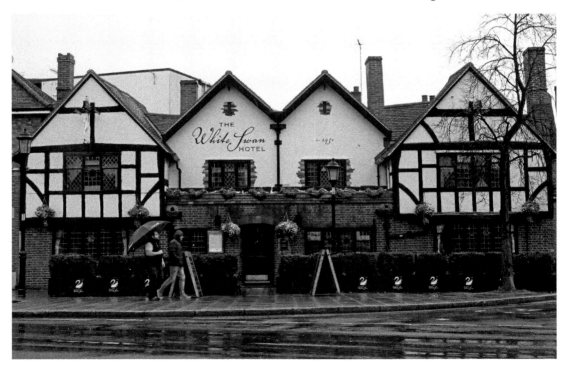

The White Swan Hotel.

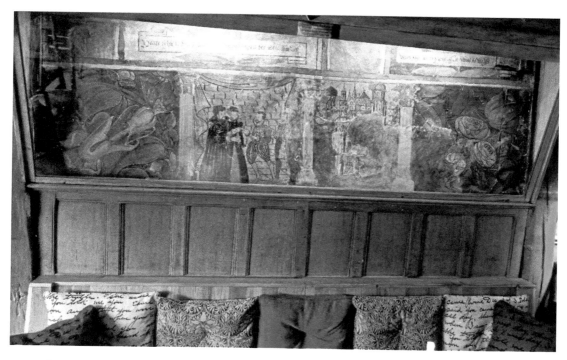

Above and right: Wall
paintings at The White Swan.

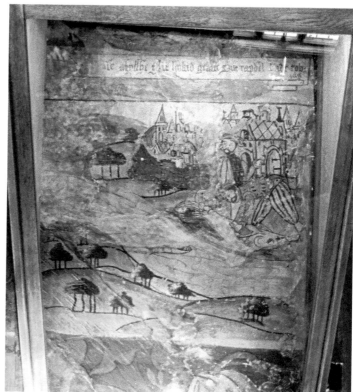

John Shakespeare, the father of the poet, who must have gazed on these murals many times, was elected. Alderman Perrott bore the council no lasting animosity, endowing an annual sermon to be preached at Holy Trinity, with provision for the burghers to 'make merye withall after the sermon is ended'.

27. The Clock Tower That Witnessed a Riot

George William Childs epitomises the rags to riches story of the American dream. Born the illegitimate son of unidentified parents in Baltimore in 1829, he was brought up by an aunt in comfortable circumstances – a fact he later downplayed in order to emphasise his remarkable rise more greatly. After a spell in the US Navy, he invested his savings in founding a publishing company in Philadelphia. He possessed huge business acumen and became very rich. It was he who devised the idea of incorporating endorsements from prominent sources on the cover of books and he was the first to launch authors on promotional tours. In 1864, he acquired Philadelphia's leading newspaper, *The Public Ledger*.

Like many self-made Americans, Childs was a noted philanthropist. As befitted a publisher, he was particularly keen on commemorating great writers, erecting memorial windows to William Cowper and George Herbert in Westminster Abbey and to John Milton at St Margaret's, Westminster, a monument to Leigh Hunt in Kensal Green Cemetery and to Edgar Alan Poe in Baltimore. His greatest gift, however, was to Stratford-upon-Avon: the American Fountain in the Rother Market, erected in honour of Queen Victoria's Golden Jubilee. This clock tower in the neo-Gothic style was built of sandstone with a granite plinth by Jethro Collins of Birmingham. It commemorates the common culture of the two nations vested in William Shakespeare. An American eagle holds a shield bearing the Stars and Stripes, while a British lion bears the royal arms. The monument provided refreshment for dogs (a bowl at the base), horses (a trough) and humans – the fountain that gives the edifice its name once had a brass drinking bowl. These facilities are now beautified by flowers rather than fulfilling their utilitarian function. There is an appropriate quote from *Timon of Athens*: 'Good honest water, which ne'er left man i' the mire' and one in praise of Shakespeare from the American writer, Washington Irving, who was himself no stranger to Stratford: 'Ten thousand honours and blessings on the bard, who has gilded the dull realities of life with innocent illusions.'

The monument was unveiled on 17 October 1887 by the great actor Henry Irving. Soon afterwards, a charming young man presented himself in the town, claiming to be Mr Childs' nephew, come to inspect his uncle's gift. He was entertained by several local worthies, relieving them of substantial loans before departing. The young man, Ernest Rolfe, had made a habit of this sort of thing and was caught attempting to play a similar trick on the Birmingham Liberal MP, Joseph Chamberlain. He received ten years' imprisonment.

The fountain became a popular place for public meetings, most notably on 16 July 1913 when fifty-six suffragists marching to London in support of votes for women

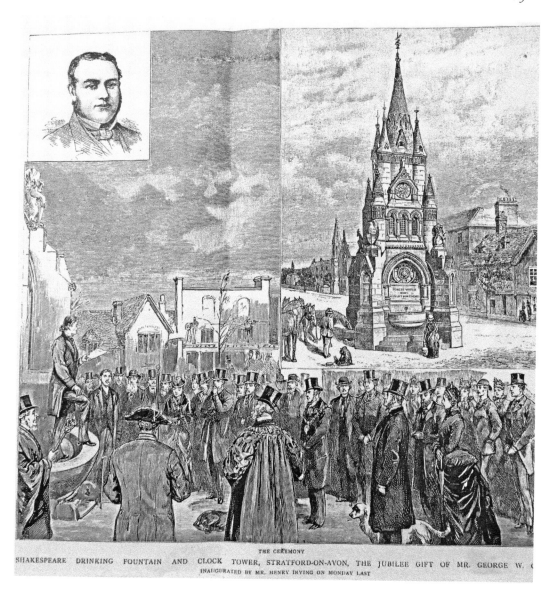

THE CEREMONY

SHAKESPEARE DRINKING FOUNTAIN AND CLOCK TOWER, STRATFORD-ON-AVON, THE JUBILEE GIFT OF MR. GEORGE W.
INAUGURATED BY MR. HENRY IRVING ON MONDAY LAST

Henry Irving unveiling the structure.

passed through Stratford and were welcomed by local supporters. They laid a wreath on Shakespeare's grave before holding a rally at the fountain. After the first speaker had welcomed the 'jolly sporting ladies', unruly spirits in the crowd started a continuous barrage of heckling. The mob surged towards the platform and several ladies were jostled. Arrests were made, but the cacophony was irrepressible. The crowd was clearly organised to prevent the speeches and the meeting was abandoned; but from another platform, the formidable Mrs Despard, a sister of the Chief of the Imperial General Staff, Sir John French, awed the remnant of the crowd into silence.

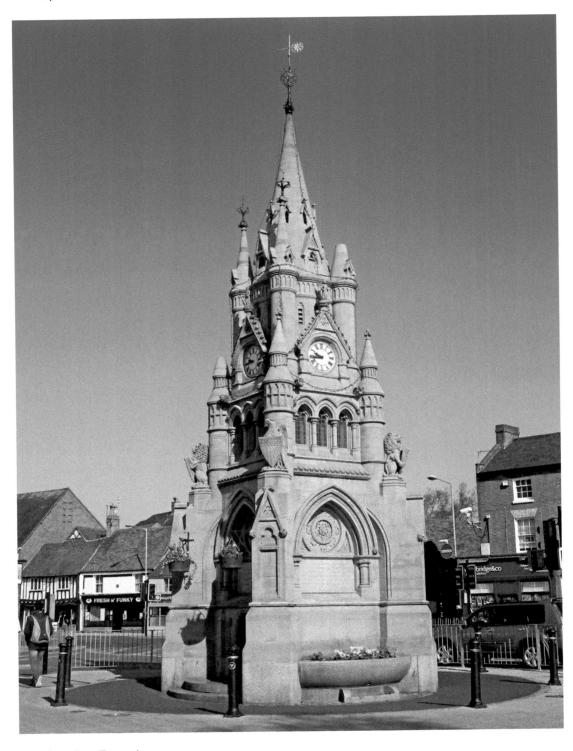

American Fountain.

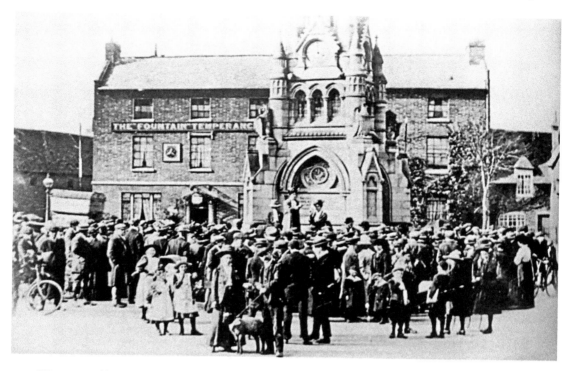

Women's suffrage meeting, 1913.

After the fountain was inaugurated, the vicar of Stratford, Revd George Arbuthnot, a fervent temperance campaigner, wrote that 'we shall do better to drink of it, rather than to patronise any of the Public Houses which abound in the town'. He took up his pen again to express shame and regret that the parish had disgraced itself by 'the violence shown by some contemptible rascals to ladies, who, whether we agree with their views or not, are peaceable citizens and entitled to that free speech, which, within the rights of the law, is the birthright of every Briton'.

28. The Pillars That Once Stood in Front of Stratford's First Theatre

A suggestion that Stratford should have its own theatre dedicated to Shakespeare was picked up by the noted comic actor Charles Mathews when he performed at the Town Hall on 10 December 1820. His show was called *A Trip to Paris* and he played all the parts in monologue. No record survives of his performance, although the correspondent of the *Warwick Advertiser* anticipated a 'delectable treat'. Yet the visit was historic for, next evening, Mathews convened a meeting at the Town Hall to consider 'the best mode of erecting, in the form of a THEATRE, a NATIONAL MONUMENT to the IMMORTAL MEMORY of SHAKESPEARE'. Mathews made a memorable speech, observing that 'the Literary and Dramatic World' had long regretted that the Birthplace of Shakespeare did not possess 'some token of NATIONAL respect and gratitude to such an immortal genius'. He appealed to the audience 'to lend their mite were it only in the gift of 5/-., as it would be the proudest boast of any person's life to say in after times when passing by this building, "Aye, I had a hand in that"'. He sat down to loud cheers. A committee was formed. Mathews selected a site in the Great Garden of New Place and an architect was appointed. Fundraising was boosted greatly by the news of Sir Walter Scott's support. The project ensured that Mathews was much seen in Stratford and performed there occasionally.

The Royal Shakespearean Theatre opened on 12 December 1830, with performances of *As You Like It* and *Catherine and Petruchio*. The décor and style of the building were much admired. Two years later the theatre received the endorsement of the greatest theatrical figures of the age when Edmund Keen played Richard III and Shylock, and W. C. Macready played Hamlet. Despite this initial success, the theatre did not thrive. In 1844 the stage and pit were removed and the building was reopened as an educational institute, the Royal

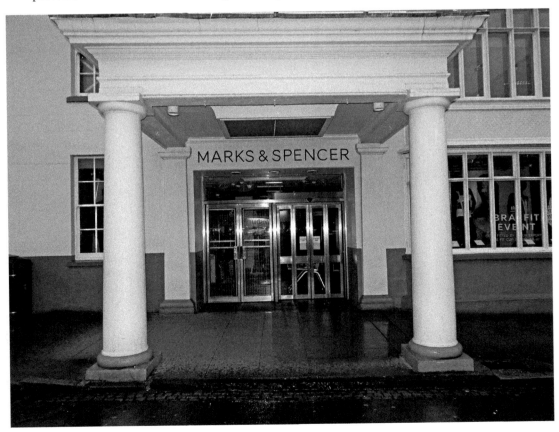

Marks & Spencer's, showing the surviving pillars.

Shakespearean Rooms. Nor was this a great success and it finally closed its doors in 1872. The building was demolished – only its portico survived. It was transferred to provide a grand entrance to the Shakespeare Hotel. Sometime before the First World War it was transferred again, this time to the Red Horse Hotel, in Bridge Street, which is now Marks & Spencers, and it still stands as a reminder of Stratford's first theatre.

29. Further Afield

The Farmhouse Bearing the Initials of Anne Hathaway's Great-Nephew
The building the world knows as Anne Hathaway's Cottage is the subject of something of a misnomer. It is actually a substantial farmhouse, the earliest part of which dates from the 1460s. Its name before the growing tourist industry gave it its twee title – Hewland's Farm – which demonstrates its original function.

The Hathaways were a family of local standing. Their prosperity may be seen in their substantial farmhouse. John Hathaway, an archer, probably Anne's grandfather, appeared on the muster roll of 1536 and later became a town constable. Anne's brother, Bartholomew, was twice churchwarden of Holy Trinity and his son, Richard, was elected bailiff in 1626. Her father, Richard Hathaway, left the considerable holdings of more than 120 acres at his death in 1581. To his daughter 'Agnes' – the name was interchangeable with Anne,

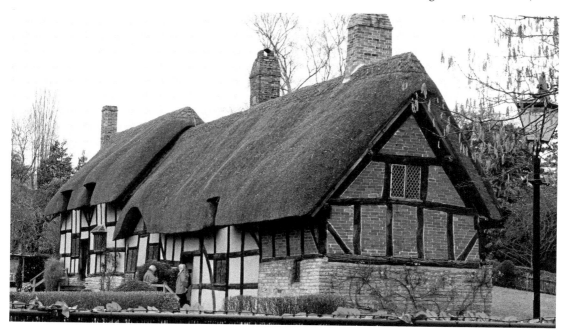

Anne Hathaway's Cottage.

the 'g' being silent in the French fashion – he left 10 marks for a dowry, expressing the hope that his chief heir, Bartholomew, would be 'a comforte unto his Brethren and Sisters to his powers'. The presumed recipient of this presumed fraternal largesse was William Shakespeare, aged eighteen. On 28 November 1582 the diocesan clerk in Worcester noted the granting of a license for a proposed match between 'William Shagspere and Anne Hathaway of Stratford'. Anne was three months pregnant at the time, which need not necessarily betoken youthful sexual incontinence, but may represent the custom of 'pre-nuptial contract', under which betrothed couples could enjoy connubial rights, but with the proviso that marriage was necessary to legitimise any potential offspring. Was William thinking of the ancestral home of the Hathaways when he wrote of Celia's house in *As You Like It*?

> West of this place, down in the neighbor bottom,
> The rank of osiers by the murmuring stream
> Left on your right hand brings you to the place.

The links between the Hathaway and Shakespeare families continued as long as William and Anne's descent. Their granddaughter and last surviving descendent, Elizabeth, left

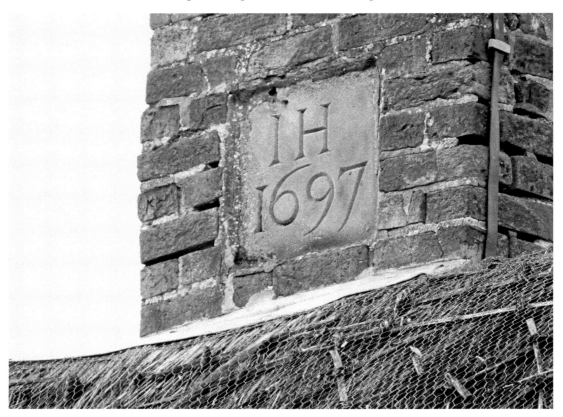

John Hathaway chimney.

bequests to the five daughters of 'my kinsman Thomas Hathaway, late of Stratford', four of whom bore the Shakespearean family names of Judith, Joan, Elizabeth and Susanna.

Anne's brother, Bartholomew, extended the house that he had inherited, adding the part of the structure nearest the orchard. His grandson made further alterations and, to record this, placed his initials 'I.H.' on the great chimney stack nearest the road and the date '1697'.

After John Hathaway died, the property passed through the female line. The last Hathaway descendent to own it was Mrs Mary Baker, who sold the property to the Shakespeare Birthday Trust in 1892. Her son, William, continued to live there rent-free until his death in 1911.

The First Building Named After Queen Victoria, Where the Creator of One of the World's Most Famous Cartoons Once Lived

On 24 May 1837, the birthday of the heiress to the throne, Princess Victoria, the Royal Victoria Spa was opened at Bishopton, a hamlet just to the north of Stratford. It had long been known to possess a spring whose water was 'very beneficial in various complaints'. The Pump Room was the first building in the area to be built in the style that became known as Victorian Gothic. There would be thousands of buildings all over the world named after Victoria, but this obscure spa was the first. Within a month of the spa's opening, the future Queen-Empress succeeded to the throne.

The spa was not a success and soon closed its doors, becoming a private house. In the early 1900s the building, which had become known as Victoria Lodge, was bought by a former Indian Army officer, Major Thomas Bairnsfather. His elder son, Bruce, was a talented artist, but it was intended that he should follow his father into the military and he was sent to the United Services College at Westward Ho! The school was instructed to beat his artistic leanings out of him. In this it failed, but the boy suffered a miserable time and, probably deliberately, failed the entrance exams for Sandhurst, so, in 1904, he was sent to Stratford's Trinity College as a weekly boarder. Here he flourished, drawing cartoons on the walls of his attic bedroom. He finally persuaded his father to allow him to attend art classes at the newly built technical college. He was greatly encouraged by the principal, who recognised his talent. In 1906 he passed his army exams and joined the 3rd Militia Royal Warwicks on a short-service commission. He found army life tedious and managed to extricate himself from it, or so he thought at the time. After enrolling in art school in London, he designed advertisements on a freelance basis – Lipton's Tea and Player's Navy Cut were among his commissions. Finding that he couldn't get enough work to support himself, he joined Spencers, a firm of electrical contractors back in Stratford. One of his tasks was to install the electrical wiring at the theatre. Each season he worked on the lighting rig for 30s a week. For the rest of the year he either worked at Flower's Brewery or travelled the country, installing electrical systems in the mansions of the wealthy, where he was generally treated as a house guest. With the declaration of war on 4 August 1914, he was recalled to a new company of Territorial Rifles as its first commander. He had been on a job for Spencers in Newfoundland. He returned home to Bishopton to find a terse note from his employers: 'Dear Sir, owing to the outbreak of European War, your services are no longer required.' He was in Belgium a few weeks later, serving in the Ploegsteert (Plug Street) Wood sector. He was appalled at the horrors of war and declined home leave

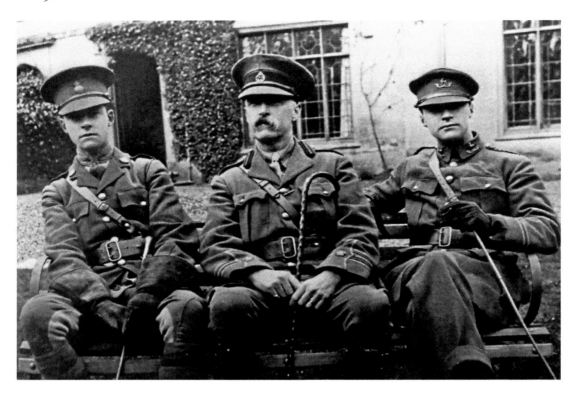

Thomas Bairnsfather with his sons Bruce and Duncan.

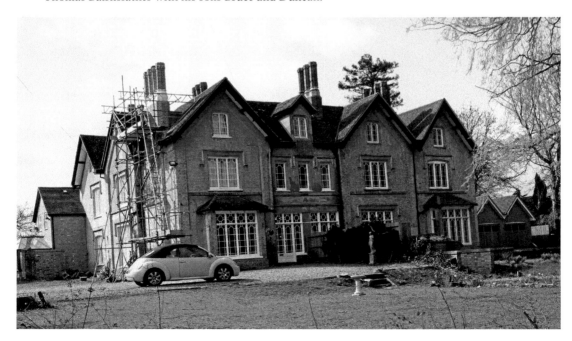

Royal Victoria Lodge.

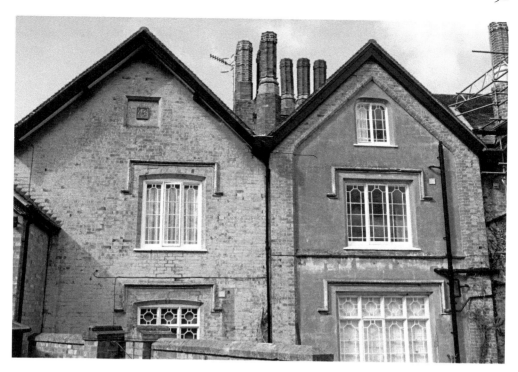

Detail of the Royal Victoria Lodge.

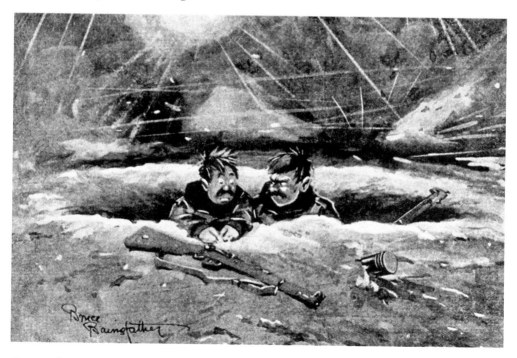

Cartoon by Bruce Bairnsfather.

because he thought that he would probably be disinclined to return. He had started to submit cartoons to the noted magazine, *The Bystander*. To his delight, they were accepted and he began to send his work on a regular basis.

Bruce Bairnsfather witnessed the spontaneous Christmas truce of 1914, which occurred in many places along the line. 'There was not an atom of hate on either side that day', he wrote. For his inaction to prevent this fraternisation, he was investigated with a view to a court martial, but it was clearly felt that he was too valuable an officer to lose. On 22 April 1915 the Germans introduced a terrible new weapon – chlorine gas. Bruce Bairnsfather was a victim of the assault. He was treated at a field station and eventually conveyed to King's College, London, where he was diagnosed as suffering from shell shock. After his discharge from hospital, he returned to Bishopton. When he recovered he was posted to the Isle of Wight to train recruits. While there he devised his cartoon character, 'Old Bill', who features in the most famous cartoon of the First World War – 'Well, if you knows of a better 'ole, go to it.'

Today, the former home of the Bairnsfathers in Bishopton is a noted B&B; a blue plaque on the wall denotes that the First World War's most celebrated artist lived there.

The House of a Gunpowder Plotter

At Michaelmas in 1605, Robert Catesby persuaded Ambrose Rookwood to take a lease on Clopton House in Stratford. Catesby was plotting nothing less than to blow up Parliament

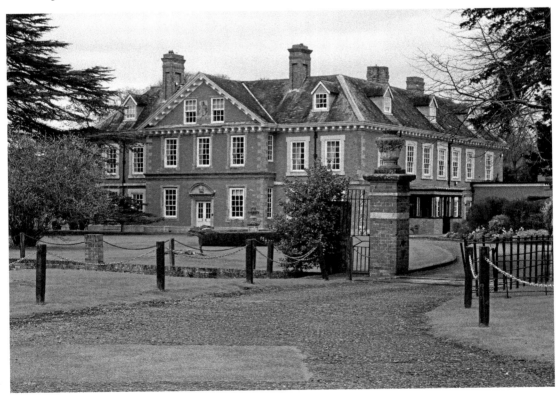

Clopton House.

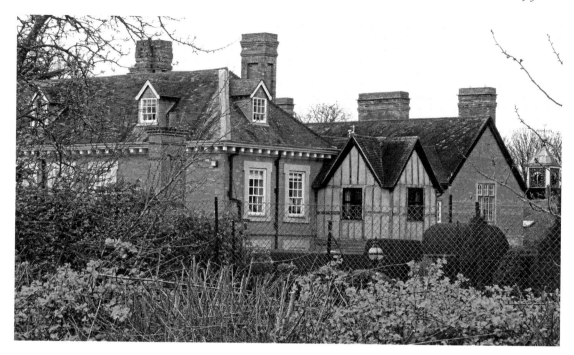

Rear view of Clopton House.

on 5 November, the day of its state opening by King James. Rookwood was a staunch Catholic who possessed estates in Suffolk and a stable of fine horses, which Catesby considered could be invaluable to the conspiracy. The house was close to those of his fellow conspirators, who were mainly impoverished local Catholic gentry. They whiled away their time 'ryding of great horses and hunting'. When the plot was discovered, Rookwood rode out of London to warn his fellow conspirators. They seized horses from Sir Fulke Greville's stables at Warwick before being besieged together at Holbeche House in Staffordshire. In the ensuing melee, Catesby was killed, but Rookwood was captured. He was put on trial with the other surviving conspirators and hung, drawn and quartered three days later.

At Stratford, the excitement was intense. The town armour was removed from its repository and repaired and replenished. Musters were raised, gunpowder purchased and tactics discussed. Wild rumours circulated. On the night of 9 November, the Corporation drank at Mrs Quiney's tavern, 'when yt was said that Sir Fulke Greville's house was besieged'.[1] The horse stealing had grown to a full campaign in just three days. An expedition was launched against Clopton House, which the local trained band was doubtless delighted to find unoccupied. Goods were seized, including chalices, surplices and other vestments.

The Monument to Manchester's First Member of Parliament
High on the Welcombe Hills, and visible for miles, stands a handsome obelisk. Few who gaze on it from afar will realise that it commemorates Manchester's first MP of the

modern era. The town (it was not a city until 1847) had lost its parliamentary representation in 1660 as a punishment for its support for Parliament during the Civil War. By the early nineteenth century, the system had become a national scandal, with rotten boroughs with few electors sending two members to the House of Commons while huge industrial centres like Birmingham and Manchester were unrepresented. The franchise represented a mere fraction of the male electorate. Pressure for change was immense and the country stood on the verge of a revolution, with rioting in the streets.

The Great Reform Act of 1832 was a relatively modest measure, which extended the franchise to 17 per cent of the adult male population and redistributed parliamentary seats away from the rotten boroughs towards the major centres. Manchester would be represented by two Members of Parliament. That December, Mark Phillips was one of those elected. The son of a wealthy merchant, he was a great supporter of the radical Anti-Corn Law League, and of such measures as the extension of schooling and the provision of public libraries. In 1841 he acquired the Welcombe estate on the outskirts of Stratford, commissioning, in 1866, the noted architect Henry Clutton to build a huge neo-Tudor mansion on the site of the old manor house. On his death in 1873, the estate passed to his brother, Robert Needham Phillips, the Liberal MP for Bury. Three years later he caused the obelisk to be erected in memory of his brother, who had made parliamentary history.

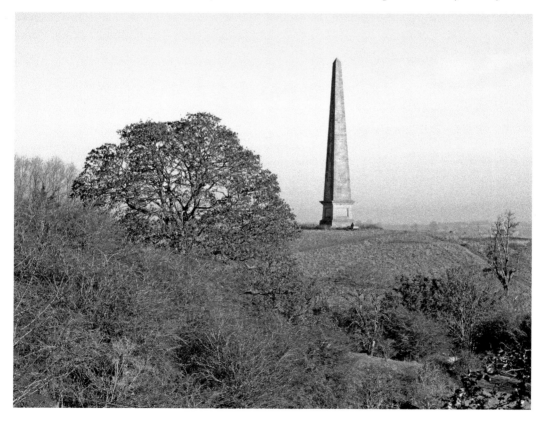

Welcombe monument.

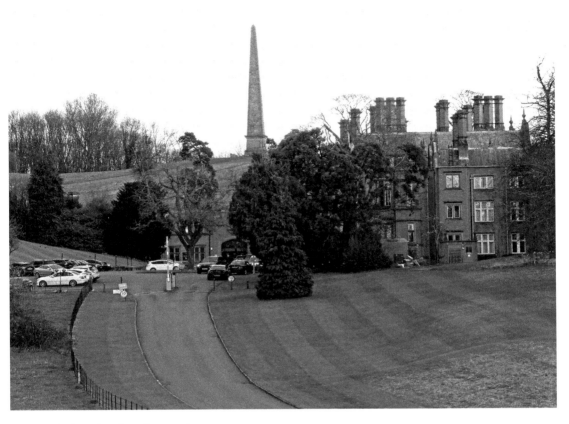

Obelisk and Welcombe Hotel.

After the death of R. N. Phillips in 1890, the Welcombe estate passed to his daughter, Caroline, the wife of Sir George Trevelyan, who served in several Liberal cabinets. On the death of his son, George Otto Trevelyan, in 1928, the mansion was bought by the London, Midland & Scottish Railway, which extended it and converted it into a hotel. It still functions as a hotel, spa and golf resort.

Notes

4. The Statue Inspired by the Divine Sarah
1. Duncan, Sophie, 'Shakespeare's Shrine', *The Oxonian Review* (November 2012).
2. Doran, Gregory, '11 Things You Didn't Know About the Bard', *Daily Telegraph* (23 April 2016).

7. The Windows Commemorating an Acting Company
1. It is now located above the bar on the ground floor.

13. Holy Trinity Church
1. The saint was especially venerated in Stratford.
2. This was the former medieval College of Priests. It was demolished in 1799.

16. The Waiter's Tab
1. The name of the Anglian tribe that settled in the area.

29. Further Afield
1. This is Shakespeare's daughter, Judith, who was married to Thomas Quiney, a vintner.